C0-AAP-107

Success in the Superintendency

Tips and Advice

Kay T. Worner

Published in partnership with the
American Association of School Administrators

ROWMAN & LITTLEFIELD EDUCATION
A division of
ROWMAN & LITTLEFIELD PUBLISHERS, INC.
Lanham • New York • Toronto • Plymouth, UK

Published in partnership with the American Association of School Administrators

Published by Rowman & Littlefield Education
A division of Rowman & Littlefield Publishers, Inc.
A wholly owned subsidiary of The Rowman & Littlefield Publishing Group, Inc.
4501 Forbes Boulevard, Suite 200, Lanham, Maryland 20706
http://www.rowmaneducation.com

Estover Road, Plymouth PL6 7PY, United Kingdom

Copyright © 2010 by Kay T. Worner

All rights reserved. No part of this book may be reproduced in any form or by any electronic or mechanical means, including information storage and retrieval systems, without written permission from the publisher, except by a reviewer who may quote passages in a review.

British Library Cataloguing in Publication Information Available

Library of Congress Cataloging-in-Publication Data

Worner, Kay T.
  Success in the superintendency : tips and advice / Kay T. Worner.
    p. cm.
  Published in partnership with the American Association of School Administrators.
  Includes bibliographical references.
  ISBN 978-1-60709-031-1 (cloth : alk. paper) — ISBN 978-1-60709-032-8 (pbk. : alk. paper) — ISBN 978-1-60709-033-5 (electronic)
  1. School superintendents—United States. 2. School management and organization—United States. I. Title.
  LB2831.72.W67 2010
  371.2'011—dc22

                                                                    2009053926

Printed in the United States of America

Contents

Foreword

Several years ago, two national position papers, *Better Leaders for America's Schools: A Manifesto* (Broad Foundation and Thomas B. Fordham Institute, 2003) and "A License to Lead? A New Leadership Agenda for America's Schools" (Hess, 2003), urged state policymakers to rescind or at least make voluntary licensing requirements for superintendents. I was invited to respond to these proposals in a monograph published by the University Council for Educational Administration. Arguing against deregulation, I posited that deregulation was both unwarranted and potentially detrimental to society (Kowalski, 2004).

Among the approximately 13,000 superintendents in the United States, most practice in small districts where they first and foremost must be education leaders—that is, professional educators providing direction for and stewarding school improvement. Moreover, allowing noneducators to serve in this pivotal position could erode the intricate balance between professionalism and democracy that has been a hallmark of this country's public education system for more than 150 years.

In large measure, attempts to deprofessionalize district and school administration are possible because of a lack of empirical data demonstrating the essential knowledge and skills required to be a superintendent. As a superintendent, I relied on two bodies of knowledge to guide me—theoretical wisdom I learned from my able professors and tacit wisdom I learned in practice and from experienced peer superintendents. Anyone who understands the demands of this challenging position accurately realizes how much one must know and do.

Contemporary superintendents concurrently are education leaders, organizational managers, democratic facilitators, applied social scientists, and effective communicators. Moreover, they face two seemingly impossible assignments: they are expected to maintain efficient schools that are at the same time highly innovative and effective, and they are expected to provide professional leadership while remaining subservient to the will of the people. Despite these complex obligations, thousands of knowledgeable and dedicated practitioners have been able to perform with distinction.

Approximately a century ago, superintendents in lighthouse districts were considered the nation's leading education scholars. Their administrative behaviors were the subject of books, journal articles, and countless conference papers. Over time, and especially after World War II, the field of educational administration struggled to legitimize itself as a social science. During this period that lasted several decades, professional publications and conferences paid less attention to crafting knowledge than they did to research. Today, however, interest in tacit knowledge has been renewed, and it is again valued by scholars and practitioners. In fact, many universities now seek to employ former practitioners as professors.

Dr. Kay Worner, as am I, is one of those former superintendents who became a professor. She now has opportunities to integrate theory and practice so that her students benefit from both. In this book, she offers insights melding her former and present professional roles. The suggestions and examples she provides will be of interest to both novice and experienced superintendents, and they are especially relevant to those who are committed to forging reforms at the local district level. The content not only addresses pertinent change strategies but also concentrates on how superintendents can build and maintain relationships with school board members and other stakeholders—associations that have become foundational to garnering the social and political capital needed to improve schools.

Theodore J. Kowalski
Professor and the Kuntz Family Endowed Chair
in Educational Administration
University of Dayton

REFERENCES

Broad Foundation & Thomas B. Fordham Institute. (2003). *Better leaders for America's schools: A manifesto.* Los Angeles: Authors.

Hess, F. M. (2003). A license to lead? A new leadership agenda for America's schools. Washington, DC: Progressive Policy Institute.

Kowalski, T. J. (2004). The ongoing war for the soul of school administration. In *Better leaders for America's schools: Perspectives on the manifesto*, ed. T. J. Lasley, 92–114. Columbia, MO: University Council for Educational Administration.

Preface

Every superintendent—new or well experienced—quickly learns that the actual job is bigger than previously described or anticipated and that support from colleague superintendents is not only helpful but also sometimes critical. The fact is superintendents need each other. No amount of preparation can truly teach the right (or best) way to approach every situation in the superintendency. The challenges are as unique as the person filling the top position in a school district. But what can assist new or aspiring superintendents is a book filled with tips and wisdom from those who are highly experienced and widely recognized for their leadership.

The purpose of this book is to provide advice and counsel with this added incentive: these tips and ideas come from Superintendents of the Year who have been honored and recognized by colleagues at the state and national levels.

THE CHALLENGE

A successful superintendent must be able to stir things up as a change agent as well as smooth whatever rough waters already exist or emerge over time. The subtitle behind the job description reads: be a master of events and nonevents. Successful superintendents are both proactive and reactive.

Early in my career, a mentor superintendent shared two reasons why I must not to be misled at any given moment by a peaceful landscape: "Your primary mission as a school superintendent is to take initiative that will improve teaching and learning, which will rarely escape resistance or outright opposition. In any case, the seeds of the next problem of your doing, or not, have already sprouted; always keep a watchful eye over your left and right shoulder."

A school superintendent faces a host of challenges, some self-initiated and others unbidden. In these matters, successful administrators often draw upon knowledge that other superintendents have acquired from firsthand experience. Collegial perspectives, skill sets, and tested abilities can be very instructive.

Many new superintendents, overwhelmed by hours on the job, promise their family that things will soon settle down, e.g., after the next board election; settlement in tense negotiations; closure to a referendum campaign; legislative session ends; and so on. Then reality hits—challenges in the superintendency never end and rarely do they repeat themselves in exactly the same way. The learning curve for successful superintendents is ever upward.

COLLEGIAL HELP

To whom should aspiring, new, and even mature school superintendents turn for help? The logical and pragmatic answer is one's colleagues. Superintendents and their colleagues face common issues, experience wins and losses, and know the agony of defeat and the joys of success.

The litany of school-related issues is so familiar because people everywhere are fairly consistent in their wants, motivations, and expectations but have infinite variety in timing and intensity. This unfolding, ever-changing human drama within a school district setting gives rise to a plethora of in-basket tasks and out-basket decisions that are faced by all superintendents.

Superintendents need each other because so much can be learned from one another! Colleagues help by describing shortcuts, pointing out pitfalls, and sharing processes that improve probability of success. Superintendents can share political astuteness gained by working with multiple constituencies, labor unions, and school board member turnover. Men and women who are successful in this top leadership position understand that their job description calls for protection of the sacred traditions of society while preparing its children for a future full of change.

Not last, nor least, superintendents have to grapple with personal issues of great magnitude: how to relish and fulfill the role but not let the job define the person in the job. A fulfilled life includes purposes that encompass not only work but also family, worship, recreation, and personal as well as professional growth. Balancing these priorities is among the greatest challenges for school superintendents.

Thus, superintendents have always communicated with one another for advice, information, and support. The linkage in nearly every case has come from a neighboring superintendent long in tooth, a superintendent friend met in graduate school, or a superintendent who shared his or her wisdom in a workshop or conference setting. Thankfully, such close-at-hand professional touchstones remain in place.

CONTRIBUTORS

However, in 1987, a new era began! The American Association of School Superintendents (AASA) embarked on a new initiative in partnership with the ServiceMaster Corporation (now ARAMARK Corporation). The mission was, and is, to identify and give long overdue recognition to school superintendents in every state whose success in local school administration as well as their contributions to the profession as a whole makes them worthy of recognition. The Superintendent of the Year program does just that.

Selection criteria over the past twenty-three years have been rigorous. Each year, the application includes the candidate's resume, letters of recommendation, school board endorsement, and answers to five essay questions that change every year to reflect current educational issues. Each state uses the same criteria and its own internal selection processes that will best meet overall program purposes.

The written applications of state winners are, in turn, forwarded to AASA where a Blue Ribbon Task Force Selection Committee reads them very carefully and selects four finalists who are invited to Washington D.C. Each speaks before the National Press Club and is interviewed individually by the same panel, whose selection for National Superintendent of the Year is not announced until the opening session of the National Superintendent of the Year.

This program has now blossomed for over two decades. Ms. Darlene Pierce has been program director since its inception. There are now over 1,000 state winners, ninety-two finalists (four per year) of that number for national recognition, and twenty-three carry the honorary title "National Superintendent of the Year."

These honored men and women represent the best knowledge, practices, and reputations within the ranks of school superintendents. Indeed, these highly respected, experienced superintendents from around the nation serve as a highly competent and trustworthy resource to aspiring and new school superintendents as well as colleagues at all stages of their career. It is many of their experiences and suggestions that this book's author opens to the reader.

A TREASURY OF TIPS AND ADVICE

The book's author and editor is Dr. Kay Worner, former State Superintendent of the Year (2004, Minnesota). She brings years of personal experience to school administration not only as a superintendent but also as a highly sought-after educational consultant, presenter, and writer. Dr. Worner is now serving as Associate Professor of Educational Administration at St. Cloud State University.

The author draws upon the resources of state and national winners within the AASA Superintendent of the Year Program to provide the Tips and Advice and Quick Tips sections of the book. This is the first effort to pull together ideas, practices, and experiences of these distinguished superintendents into one place for the benefit of new or aspiring superintendents as they begin their journey.

WHAT YOU WILL DISCOVER

This book provides practical, common-sense advice in ten chapters organized by typical issues facing superintendents. It is not theory oriented, nor is the book filled with self-aggrandizement. Instead, it provides tips and advice for each chapter topic from some of America's most distinguished superintendents.

The reader will recognize that the critical issues covered in the book are those that are eventually faced by all superintendents. The format aids quick reference and understanding. Best of all, tips and advice come from colleagues who have vast, firsthand experience. The book will be a valued resource to many, whether an aspiring or new superintendent, a professor of school administration, or a superintendent in later stages of the professional journey.

Dr. Donald Draayer
National Superintendent of the Year, 1990

Acknowledgments

This book is definitely an accomplishment of many. Literally dozens of people supported, influenced, contributed, assisted, and/or tolerated me over the last eighteen months while I worked on the book. The book would not exist if the contributors were not willing to share their thoughts, ideas, experience, expertise, tips, and advice. They make the book unique and practical.

The group that originally had the idea for the book is the Executive Committee of the Minnesota Association of School Administrators. When they contacted me and suggested that I consider writing a book about the superintendency, the process began. Minnesota is proud to have two National Superintendents of the Year, Dr. Don Draayer, 1990, and Dr. Kenneth Dragseth, 2003. These two gentlemen provided excellent guidance and counsel to me for the book, its structure and format. Their advice was stellar; I feel honored to have them both as colleagues, friends, and mentors.

My colleagues, Dale Gasser, Greg Vandal, Jim Rickabaugh, Don Helmstetter, Ben Kanninen, and Ted Blaesing, took a chance on the book by writing their Tips and Advice for chapter 1. Their work is the reason the proposal was accepted.

My immediate family members are my motivation and my inspiration. They are acknowledged for their patience and understanding of Mom's (or Grandma's) preoccupation with "The Book." My sister-in-law, Marilyn Worner, provided invaluable editing skills that spurred me on to further editing changes and improvements.

Chapter 1 of the book is called "Leading with Integrity." I selected that title for the first chapter because I believe it is the most important topic of all the chapters. As a daughter of hardworking, Midwestern, supportive parents, I was taught to value integrity as a personal and professional quality. I learned from my father that behaving with integrity is more important than accumulating money or success. How you treat others is more important than your job title. My mother passed away in 2001; my father in 2008 at age ninety. Their life lessons live on.

I acknowledge and thank my colleagues Drs. Janine Dahms-Walker, Frances, Kayona, and Nick Miller for their support and understanding of the time I needed to spend on writing. I thank Anne Chelin-Anderson, my graduate assistant, who provided technology support.

It goes without question that the person to whom I owe the biggest debt of gratitude is my husband, Roger. He provided a calming influence when my self-imposed deadlines failed to be reached. He was my sounding board for ideas, chapter content, and overall book design. He gave excellent advice when I needed it and even when I thought I didn't. He is my mentor, my friend, my love, and my role model. He is the consummate educator, leader, consultant, superintendent, and professor. I owe him deep and heartfelt gratitude for his wisdom, intellect, and expertise.

And, I acknowledge all of the men and women who work every day to make a difference in the lives of children, their students. I have watched miracles occur, the impossible become possible, the disenfranchised become great successes, all because of the dedication, knowledge, caring, and perseverance of teachers and administrators.

Chapter One

Leading with Integrity

Integrity is one of the most important topics in leadership today. Among the many personal and professional qualities of a superintendent sought after by school boards, honesty and integrity are listed in nearly every profile of desired qualifications. The superintendent who has a reputation of having personal and professional integrity is a highly sought after candidate.

UNDERSTAND THE IMPORTANCE OF INTEGRITY

Doing the right thing for the right reason—even when no one is looking—is a simple definition of integrity. Trusted and respected leaders are those who are known for their honesty and moral "fiber." It is particularly important for leaders in public service, i.e. superintendents, to display both personal and professional integrity—the public demands it. Unfortunately, too many examples of "bad" leader behavior are splashed across headlines on a daily basis. Politicians, educators, and religious leaders in particular draw media attention and public outrage when they use questionable tactics or make decisions that are clearly self-centered and negatively impact on others.

It is difficult to know if more people in leadership positions today lack integrity than in the past. Perhaps the media is more adept at finding and exposing questionable behavior in "real time." Regardless, lack of personal or professional integrity casts a dark shadow on leadership in general. As a result, the public is more skeptical than ever about the motives of those in top level positions.

Behaving with the utmost personal and professional integrity as a superintendent is not only important, it is essential. Cottrell (2005) said, "Guard your integrity as though it is your most precious personal possession—because that

1

is exactly what it is" (p. 47). Doing the right thing for the right reason is the only way superintendents can build trust with the school community. Without trust, there is little or no support from the school community—something essential for a highly effective educational system for students.

EXPECT POSITION ACCOUNTABILITY

Few CEO-level positions hold the same high level of positions accountability as does the superintendency. Expectations for job performance the duties associated with the position are both increasing. Superintendents must be instructional leaders, excellent communicators, facility, food service, and transportation managers, astute business officials, strategic planners, human resource experts, legal analysts, policy administrators, data gatherers, motivators, community leaders, politicians, media experts, problem-solvers, negotiators, and student advocates.

Superintendents must also be knowledgeable on a variety of topics such as special education, community partnerships, early childhood programming, technology, alternative education, governance, continuous improvement/reform, marketing, and team building. This is not a position for the faint of heart or for those who lack confidence in their own abilities.

Successful superintendents understand and accept this high level of position accountability; more importantly, they are unwilling to compromise personal and professional integrity in the performance of these complex and challenging duties. Leading with integrity provides the foundation for a well-regarded, supported school system which, in turn, benefits all students.

WORK TO ESTABLISH TRUST

John Maxwell (2003) stated "If a good reputation is like gold, then having integrity is like owning the mine" (p. 62). Integrity drives decisions, builds trust, and allows others to support (or not support) decisions for their value rather than for the motive behind making the decision in the first place. Those who lead with integrity weigh their actions against principle, not ego. Leading with integrity requires asking the question, "How will this benefit others, add value to students, and help accomplish the mission of the organization?" rather than, "How does this affect me?"

Northouse (2007) said that, "Leaders with integrity inspire confidence in others because they can be trusted to do what they say they are going to do" (p. 20). Integrity and trust are inextricably bound to each other.

SHARE BELIEFS AND VALUES

Personal and professional values and beliefs help define character. It is important that the school community knows the core values and beliefs of its superintendent. If these are clear, then there is greater understanding among the school community of why and how decisions are made. Trust in the superintendent's leadership is often the result of consistent, value-based decision-making.

If a superintendent does not share core values and beliefs with the school community, decisions may appear to be arbitrary with no basis or rationale. Superintendents who display a "fundamental consistency" between values, goals, words, and actions will gain the trust and respect of the school community much faster than those who say the right thing but whose actions make the words ring hollow (Evans, 2007, p.137).

The ideal situation, for both the superintendent and the school community, is when core values and beliefs—especially about the mission of education—are similar. The superintendent who leads with integrity knows his/her own beliefs and values well. These provide their moral compass guiding attitude, behavior, and ultimately, decisions.

RECOGNIZE TESTS OF LEADERSHIP

It is often seemingly insignificant issues that test the integrity of a superintendent. A special request from a teacher or board member to place his or her child in a certain class can create a difficult situation for even the most seasoned superintendent, particularly if the request requires a privilege not extended to all. Acquiescence to special requests can have far reaching implications if others perceive the superintendent's decision as an act of favoritism or worse, an inability to withstand pressure. Doing the right thing requires courage and willingness to stand up for ethical behavior knowing there may be potential fallout—even if it means disappointing powerful or influential people. Special interest groups, school boards (or individual school board members), vociferous parents, union issues, state and national mandates, and limited resources test the fundamental character of superintendents virtually every day as they perform their duties.

Even the most optimistic, seasoned superintendents have moments of doubt about how effective they can be against the barrage of so many issues that interfere with the mission and goals of the organization. Experienced (and savvy) superintendents understand that these issues—political, social, moral, legal, and economic—affect and influence their leadership and effectiveness.

Those who stay true to the mission of educating all children seem to be able to better resist the tug and pull of outside distraction. Outside influences, some very powerful, test a superintendent's leadership ability; how the superintendent reacts to these influences reveals his/her character.

VALUE RELATIONSHIPS

The quality of the relationships superintendents have with their board, staff, students, parents and the stakeholders often determines the level of trust and respect given by the school community. These relationships are influenced by how well the superintendent listens, follows through with commitment, and responds to those seeking advice or resolution of conflict. A critical ability for a successful superintendent is to effectively separate issues from emotions. Even critical commentary can usually be delivered by staying focused on the issue rather than making it personal.

A genuine respect for human dignity is integral to establishing and maintaining good, positive relationships with the school district community. Small actions (how he/she responds to others) tell a great deal about the character of the superintendent. If integrity is about doing the right thing, then doing the right thing means valuing, respecting, and appreciating the role of every person in the school community.

MODEL INTEGRITY

Leading with integrity requires the superintendent to model these behaviors:

- doing what's right, not what's popular,
- being a lifelong learner,
- seeing strengths in others and encouraging them to be the best they can be,
- reflecting on one's own actions and decisions,
- seeing the big picture and how everything and everyone is connected,
- being a mentor and teacher,
- passing the credit and taking the blame,
- thinking through the impact—short and long range—of decisions,
- recognizing the importance of trust,
- listening to understand,
- knowing one's own personal and professional limits,
- using the expertise of others,
- being genuine and sincere,

- being visible,
- talking about education, children, and human dignity,
- acting on behalf of children and their education,
- adhering to beliefs and principles that are just,
- planning ahead for optimal success,
- being fair and consistent but not rigid,
- being humble,
- following through,
- serving as a model for others through word, action, and deed,
- recognizing the value of collective minds, and
- caring more about doing the right thing than about job security.

Leading with integrity is diminished by these behaviors:

- making arbitrary decisions,
- displaying favoritism,
- having a lack of purpose,
- applying rules inconsistently,
- needing recognition,
- failing to recognize the value of everyone in the school community,
- avoiding face to face meetings with staff, students, parents and the community at large,
- lacking courage to make tough decisions,
- succumbing to pressure from threatening (or important) people or groups,
- bending ethics,
- ignoring poor, ineffective, or inappropriate job performance of employees,
- failing to talk about importance of educating all children,
- failing to advocate for the disenfranchised,
- being vague about what is valued in the school community,
- avoiding problems and conflict,
- failing to plan,
- failing to be a mentor,
- failing to follow through with commitments, and
- placing greater value on keeping one's job than doing what's right.

ESSENCE OF INTEGRITY

No other character quality besides integrity has as much influence on how successful a superintendent is in the eyes of the school community. The smallest deviation from ethical behavior is all that is needed for trust to be destroyed and all of the positive efforts made to that point disregarded. People are unforgiving of leaders who are unethical or dishonest—particularly of those in public service. Leader integrity allows the organization to move forward and focus on its mission rather than on the behavior of the leader.

TIPS AND ADVICE

Tip: Follow Administrator's Code of Ethics

One of the most important responsibilities of a superintendent is to form a bond with district and building administrators. If an administrator fails to exemplify the personal or professional integrity necessary and expected in a leadership role, the superintendent must take appropriate and unbiased action to emphasize the importance of integrity in leadership. Friendship, length of service, or past "good works" of an administrator do not change the superintendent's responsibility to take action against a subordinate administrator who violates the administrator code of ethics.

Example:

A school district business manager noticed that $8,000 had been withdrawn from a district account with no paper trail to identify the reason for the withdrawal or for what the money was used. The business manager alerted the superintendent about the issue. Initially, no conclusion could be drawn regarding impropriety, but the account was under the direct supervision of one district-level administrator.

The superintendent asked the administrator in charge of the budget area to come to his office. The financial documents were shown to the administrator; the superintendent asked if the administrator had knowledge about the issue or an explanation. The administrator admitted taking the money to fund a home improvement project that had run over budget. He stressed that he did intend to eventually return it. The administrator was a professional colleague, a periodic social friend of the superintendent, and an active, respected leader in state and national associations of which the administrator was a member. At this point, the superintendent believed he had three options: suspend the administrator and turn the situation over to local authorities; allow the administrator to return the money and consider the issue closed; ask for restitution and the resignation of the administrator with no further action taken.

The superintendent told the administrator that his preference for the resolution of the issue was the third option. The administrator agreed and tendered his resignation at the end of the day. A cashier's check in the full amount of what was missing from the budget was mailed to the superintendent two days later. The superintendent was able to maintain confidentiality of the issue.

Advice:

Leading with integrity means that a code of ethics needs to be followed—even when it involves friends or colleagues. Personal and professional integrity is not situational.

Tip: Playing Favorites Has Consequences

Superintendent colleagues sometimes ask for favors that test leader integrity. At these times, a choice may be necessary between maintaining a relationship with a colleague and acting with personal and professional integrity.

Example:

A superintendent was approached by a neighboring superintendent with a request to consider his wife for a teaching position in his colleague's school district. At first it was assumed that he just wanted to have her candidacy considered, something the superintendent agreed to do. The wife's credentials were sent, and the superintendent passed them along to the Human Resources Office with a note asking that she be considered in light of the hiring criteria and other candidates.

A few weeks later at a conference, the neighboring superintendent approached his colleague superintendent and wanted to know why his wife was not offered the position. He also said that since he was aware another position for which his wife was licensed was available, his colleague should place his wife into that position. It quickly became clear that the neighboring superintendent did not just want his wife considered for a position but rather expected his colleague to hire his wife.

Obviously, granting this request would circumvent an established hiring process and the superintendent's commitment to ensure that the best teachers would be hired to teach students in his district. The superintendent believed that to do what the neighboring superintendent wanted him to do would be a clear ethical violation and would destroy the trusting relationship he had with the school board and community.

When the superintendent refused to commit to hiring his wife, the superintendent reacted with surprise. He claimed that where he lived previously, such a favor was commonplace and that superintendents there knew how to take care of each other. Unfortunately, the professional relationship between these two superintendents never recovered.

Advice:

Doing the right thing for the right reason can result in lost friendships, but it produces greater trust and respect where it really counts.

Tip: Some Decisions Are in the Gray Area

A superintendent must always attempt to keep his/her school district safe from any risk and, at the same time, keep the best interests of the children and the staff close to his/her heart. To do both may require flexibility and creativity. Some leadership decisions fall into the "gray area"—the outcome is not necessarily all that clear.

Example:

A superintendent received a letter from the Internal Revenue Service stating that a teacher's wages were to be garnished because of unpaid federal taxes. That same day, the superintendent was informed by the State Licensing Board that the teacher's license was to be suspended for the same violations. The superintendent knew that this teacher, who had a wife and four young children, would simply not be able to survive economically without his pay-check. Furthermore, the reputation of the popular middle school teacher in this small community would likely be irreparably tarnished if rash actions were taken. The superintendent learned that the teacher owned a fledgling business, but he had not been reporting business revenue to the IRS. In contrast to the teacher's excellent ability to teach students and maintain accurate and organized records, he failed miserably at the record-keeping aspect in his business.

In a meeting with the superintendent, the teacher acknowledged his plight and further admitted his deep depression and suicidal thoughts resulting from the issue. The superintendent placed him on paid medical leave and had him make two phone calls from the superintendent's office. The first was to an employee-assistance representative who set up an appointment later that day between a well-qualified counselor and the teacher. The second was to a cer-tified public accountant who arranged to meet with the teacher several times over the next two weeks.

The superintendent called the Teacher Licensing Board and asked them to reconsider their suspension of the license if the teacher could get his financial affairs in order to the satisfaction of the IRS. The teacher was able to do so about a month later. Because of that, and because of the arrangements made among the CPA, the teacher, and the IRS, the Board of Teaching reinstated his license.

In this situation, the Board of Teaching was satisfied, the IRS was satisfied, and the students had virtually uninterrupted quality instruction from a favorite teacher. The school district not only retained a quality teacher but also did so humanely. Whether the superintendent used the correct leadership approach or not may be debatable. It may be what is called a "gray area" decision.

Note: Just a few years later, the teacher learned he had brain cancer and ultimately succumbed to the disease. No one ever knew of the special arrangement he and the superintendent had made. No one ever needed to.

Advice:

The right thing to do may be in the "gray area" but can result in the most beneficial and humane outcome for everyone concerned.

Tip: Give Credit, Take Blame

Good leaders support the work of those around them. They create the focus and provide direction. They also are flexible and value those who are creative in their roles and responsibilities. Effective leaders mentor their subordinate staff and sometimes need to take the blame for their mistakes. Passing the credit and taking the blame is simply a part of leadership.

Example:

A relatively inexperienced secondary principal learned the last week of summer vacation that the school's only Spanish teacher resigned. Knowing the situation, an elementary principal in a neighboring school contacted the secondary principal to tell him that he had just interviewed a candidate for an educational assistant position who speaks fluent Spanish. The principal contacted the candidate and offered her the vacant Spanish position. The candidate accepted and began work the following week.

Six weeks into the year, it was discovered that the newly hired Spanish teacher was unlicensed and had a criminal record. Further investigation revealed that the principal, in the rush of events at the start of school, failed to forward hiring documents to the Human Resources Department, which would have triggered both a background and license check.

The problems inherent in the above-described situation are obvious. Clearly, the principal made a mistake, the consequences of which were quite serious. The easy course of action for the superintendent would be to blame the principal, but, ultimately, the superintendent believed the responsibility for the problem was his. In this situation, the superintendent did accept the responsibility for not assuring the hiring process was followed. Privately, the superintendent met with the principal and clarified the hiring process—a needed lesson for the principal who may have dodged a "bullet" on this one but definitely felt some of the impact.

Advice:

Leadership is not about self-aggrandizement—it is about empowering others and letting them shine. It is also about teaching others to follow process even under pressure to work around the process.

Tip: Don't Shy Away From Difficult Issues

Sometimes the only way to tackle an issue is to meet it head-on. This can be especially true in working with the media. Taking the lead in providing information and properly framing the facts of a difficult event goes a long way in controlling the damage to a district's image and reputation.

Example:

A district had been struggling for years to overcome the devastating impact of an off-campus act of violence. The attack, which resulted in the death of the victim, received a great deal of media attention. Due to the tenor of the coverage, the district's reputation as a safe and orderly place for learning suffered immensely. Just when the public image seemed to improve, another act of violence occurred—also resulting in a fatality. Even though the student who perpetrated the violence was new to the district, there was no doubt that blame for fostering and promoting violent behavior would quickly surface in media coverage.

The superintendent called for a meeting with the major media outlets in the region just before the word was out that the student in question would face criminal charges. The superintendent shared all the information that he could and still comply with the Data Privacy Act. Access to important details was provided that allowed the media to put together their breaking news stories. Because the superintendent was able to frame the information in its proper context, the reports focused on the facts of the event and not upon the district. The school system was able to avert a second crippling blow to its reputation. Just one year following this sad event, a survey indicated that the public rated "a safe and caring environment for students" as the district's top quality.

Advice:

Knowing that an issue is likely to be aired publicly, the best course of action is to take a frontal approach and provide whatever factual information that can legally be shared with the media and with the public. Too many leaders sound too much like "bureaucrats" when working with the media.

Tip: Courage and Integrity Often Go Hand-in-Hand

Sometimes having integrity as a leader means having the courage to do the right thing—especially when not everyone agrees with a decision. When confronted with high-profile decisions, integrity is placed under a microscope—a very public microscope—with the media very anxious to reveal/judge the final outcome.

Example:

In a small, rural, Midwest town, the senior class had earned a less-than-positive reputation among the teaching and administrative staff. As would be expected, the first-year principal issued stern warnings to students about proper behavior on the upcoming senior trip. During the trip, twelve senior boys wandered off and enjoyed several bottles of beer. Students had been forewarned that anyone who violated the "no alcohol" rule would be recommended for expulsion. In that state at that time, expulsion meant a total exclusion from school and hence no possible avenue to complete diploma requirements. As a result of the violation, the part-time superintendent and the principal recommended that the students be suspended from school for the remainder of the school year and banned from participation in commencement activities.

The word soon passed through the town about the decision the superintendent and principal made regarding the senior boys. Threats of violence began to be issued from a variety of sources, enough so that police escorts were needed for school administrators to and from school. As expected, a very large and angry crowd attended the next school board meeting to voice their protest about the decision barring the group to participate in commencement. At the same time, a court injunction was issued, stopping the school district from barring the students from commencement. The district appealed the injunction and was granted a hearing.

The drama from the school board meeting was reenacted in the courtroom. The judge directed the school board to conduct another hearing and either reaffirm or dismiss its previous decision to uphold the recommended suspension from school and participation in commencement. One more very emotional meeting was held in a packed school library, and the board, at the end of a long evening, affirmed their previous decision.

Graduation night came and extensive law enforcement was obvious throughout the school and community. Heightened security was needed because of the threats of violence but also because the commencement speaker was the newly elected governor. Fortunately, graduation went relatively smoothly. Most of the young men involved in the incident came as a group into the gym but then left (a silent protest) when diplomas were handed out.

As time went on, the young men completed assignments and received their diplomas. Some were contrite; a few remained combative. A few months later, the father of one of the boys approached the superintendent. Surprisingly, he extended his hand and told him that he did the right thing by standing firm against community pressure. With a shaking voice he recounted a horrific accident involving his daughter on graduation night a few years earlier that involved teens drinking and driving. He went on to say that communities need to take a stand for what is in the long-term best interest of young people.

Advice:

The pressure to change a decision can be very strong. Standing firm on a decision clearly made for the benefit of all students and for the right reason is the only course of action that builds trust, respect, and community support. Courage is often synonymous with integrity.

Chapter Two

Keeping the Focus

Public schools are people-intensive businesses. They are characterized by person-to-person interaction between and among employees, students, parents, and community members. These interactions are further intensified by the rapid access to information through the Internet and handheld communication devices. At the center of the interaction/communication network is the school district's chief executive officer—the superintendent.

It is the superintendent who is charged with the responsibility of maintaining organizational focus amid legitimate pressures to pull the organization in one fitful direction after the next. It is not uncommon that the chasing of every emerging crisis can become a pattern of operation. Clearly, however, organizations without focus are less effective and efficient in achieving strategic goals. Burke (2008) states that, "It is the leader who articulates and brings together the external environment with the organizational mission, strategy, and culture and then provides a vision for the future: the destination, the change goal(s)" (p. 225).

Early in tenure, the new superintendent should take essential steps to determine what are or should be the school district's priority focuses. The superintendent is responsible for communicating those priorities, keeping the organization on track, and keeping the focus on what has been determined as important to the district's students.

KNOW THE MISSION

Superintendents are expected to be visionary leaders. This means that the superintendent is responsible for moving the district school community forward with a vision and mission in mind. The vision describes the way the district will look and operate in the future; the mission guides the work of the district on a day-to-day basis to achieve the vision. For example, the vision of a district may be to assure that all students have access to the necessary programs and services that allow them to be successful students and productive world citizens. The mission is to maintain, enhance, and continuously improve the structure and delivery of programs and services so that every student reaches predetermined academic and developmental goals.

If the school community has not clearly articulated what they want its schools to be like and look like, then the superintendent can and should facilitate the activity leading to that outcome. This is the first step in keeping the focus.

ASSESS DISTRICT STRENGTHS AND NEEDS

As soon as possible, even during the transition time to the position, the new superintendent can and should seek information about the organization's strengths and weaknesses. The National School Boards Association in their Strategic Planning Toolkit for School Board and Superintendents (2009) calls this process taking stock. This is best accomplished by investing time in interviewing key district stakeholders, including: district and building administrators, school board members, union leadership, parents and district residents, government officials, and, if possible, a sampling of high school students. The twenty- to thirty-minute individual interview allows the superintendent to ask: "What are the district's strengths? What are the weaknesses or concerns? What is the highest priority issue that needs to be addressed in the near future?" This interview process provides a quick indication of themes, issues, and needs and district strengths. Some of theses issues may be relatively small in scope and simple, but others large in scope and quite complex. Regardless, previously unknown information to the superintendent is likely to be uncovered.

USE THE ADMINISTRATIVE TEAM

The early creation of an administrative team is requisite to gathering more detailed data on organizational needs, the details of those needs, and their prioritization. The administrative team is also instrumental in developing direction (action plans) and assisting the superintendent in maintaining focus on solving problems.

The administrative team is typically comprised of individuals who have significant roles in the leadership of departments or divisions critical to school and district operations. Team members are immediately subordinate to the superintendent. They serve in the superintendent's "inner circle" because of their knowledge of the district and their intelligence, confidentiality, loyalty, and expertise. For each of their respective departments or areas of responsibility, they maintain their own team structure that, in its own right, is a dynamic, problem-solving, communicating unit supporting administrative team decisions.

This organizational structure is of tremendous assistance to the superintendent in keeping the focus on the highest priority issues and developing the plans that assure the focus leads to productive results or outcomes. It is through the administrative team that the superintendent, with counsel and advice from the team members, delineates the issues deserving priority attention and the greatest investment of human and capital resources.

DEVELOP A COMMUNICATION NETWORK

During the early and subsequent stages of needs identification, the new superintendent communicates findings on a regular basis to the school board, administrative team, and other district stakeholders as warranted. Input opportunities are provided for those who wish to weigh in on the information provided. Whether input from district stakeholders is actually received or not, the open communication system provided by the superintendent is welcomed and respected. Furthermore, given that the identified needs outlined by the superintendent actually arose out of interviews with many district personnel and patrons, stakeholders can take heart in the knowledge that they were heard.

The goals and priorities of the district are a focus in nearly every district communication document. If a superintendent wants to maintain energy and progress toward important initiatives, the goals and priorities are the items that receive attention at school board meetings, administrative team meetings, parent meetings, and in the many communication vehicles available to the schools and district office. Since highest priority issues are small in number, or should be, it is not difficult to keep stakeholders involved in what those issues are and how the district is doing in meeting those priority goals.

The superintendent has (or can have) the ear of virtually everyone in the district. When he or she speaks, people listen. Therefore, when the superintendent talks about strengths, areas of promise, and areas of priority, those who hear begin to understand what the district is working toward and why. The more defined and extensive the communication network is, the more likely the superintendent can gain support for the efforts of the organization to address its most pressing issues.

PLAN STRATEGICALLY TO MEET PRIORITIES

With clear vision, an agreed-upon mission, and high-priority needs identified, the superintendent is well positioned to create or cause to create planning groups, task forces, or a broadly based strategic planning process—whichever seems most appropriate for the district.

The planning groups or task forces are charged with specifying a range of alternative approaches and strategies for attacking the need (or needs). In the final analysis, the preferred strategy—with greatest promise for success in addressing the need—is selected. Once the strategy is agreed upon, the next step is to develop the plan of action. The plan of action is a step-by-step procedural road map for implementing the selected strategy. It details a series of tasks that need to be accomplished. Each task is assigned, by name, to a responsible district staff member with dates for completion listed.

The last step of the action plan is reporting on and evaluating progress. Although this step is included in many plans, it is frequently omitted or ill defined. Unless the evaluative procedures are articulated and final outcomes are reported to a designated person or persons, the impact of the planning process is never really known. It is critical that the results of the strategic planning process are transmitted to the superintendent and administrative team for review and fine-tuning.

In small districts, it is likely that the superintendent would be in charge of the strategic planning process. In very large districts, a facilitator is often used to keep the task forces or planning groups on target with developing plans of action.

FOCUS ON THE PLAN

Depending on the nature and impact of the strategic planning process initiated by the superintendent, he or she may want to formally institutionalize the strategic initiatives, setting into motion organizational change. The plan can be brought to the school board with a request for formal board approval. In this instance, the initiative—including the needs to be addressed, strategy, plans of action, tasks, and time lines—has the weight of organizational policy.

An alternative approach is to bring the plan to the school board as an informational item without the call for school board action. This still allows the superintendent to proceed with the implementation of the plan to address the highest priority needs and to communicate progress on the action plans to district and community stakeholders. This approach is a less formal way to conduct strategic planning, but it can still result in systemic changes or improvements. The superintendent determines to what extent the strategic initiatives should be board sanctioned and board driven.

Whether board sanctioned or not, strategic goals should be tailored for the students in the district. Superintendents quickly learn that the "one size fits all" approach to strategic planning is a meaningless activity. Superintendents avoid using district resources (personnel, time, and monetary) on the development of a plan that could very well have been developed for any district anywhere. Plans that are not specific are not helpful, and they cannot produce systemic change required to move the district forward to better serve its student population. A generic type of plan, once completed, often sits on a shelf as a constant reminder of the waste of time and money.

The strategic planning process is critical for maintaining focus on students and their success. But strategic planning efforts cannot be effective if they do not address the highest priority needs of the students and the district. These priorities give the plan the substance and the meaning needed for staff, school board, and community buy-in.

It is the job of the superintendent to make sure time, energy, and resources are going toward these high-priority areas of students and school community. Those areas provide direction in the organization and, ultimately, benefit the students. The best plans focus on evidence-based blueprints that serve as a foundation for all strategies and activities. They allow school improvement efforts to be individualized and accountable for producing the desired results (Knoff, 2009).

The results of the planning process provide direction for change—change that is specific, targeted, and effective in producing the desired results. As difficult as change is for any organization, strategic planning takes some of the "bite" out of the belief that change is to be avoided.

Mintzberg (1994) believes that planning is about creativity, not rearranging old ideas. He was concerned that change often results in nothing new, nothing creative or different. Meaningful change takes place when the manager/leader is a strategic thinker who synthesizes strategic planning information to create a new vision for future direction and develops new strategies for achieving the vision. Leaders who become too immersed in the planning process may stifle the development of these new strategies. Mintzberg (1994) also believes that leaders should synthesize information/data and not be the actual data gatherer.

The planning process is essential for addressing the issues that need the most attention. But not every issue can be incorporated into the strategic plan. In fact, there are a multitude of those types of issues in every school district because not all initiatives are of high priority but still need attention. A new superintendent cannot fix every issue that requires fixing; there simply is not enough time in his/her day. Therefore, these issues are most often those brought to the administrative team agenda for review and discussion. The administrative team structure provides the vehicle for the superintendent to empower subordinate administrators to tackle some of the issues that need fine-tuning outside of the main strategic plan goals.

ESSENCE OF KEEPING THE FOCUS

As in the case of an orchestra where the conductor is responsible for maintaining the focus for the entire body of musicians, so, too, is the superintendent charged with keeping a harmonic balance of the component parts of a complex enterprise. The superintendent keeps the strategic plan and its implementation on task, on target, and on time in addressing priority organizational needs. It is an awesome responsibility but doable with the help of personnel and process tools that are at the superintendent's disposal.

TIPS AND ADVICE

Tip: Look at the Existing Strategic Plan Before Starting Over

The strategic planning process can be valuable to a new superintendent. A well-developed plan helps focus time, energy, and resources on select issues. The strategic planning process can be a lengthy grassroots effort involving many people or consist of a short review of an existing plan. How extensive the planning process is for a new superintendent depends on the quality and usefulness of the plan already in place.

Example:

A new superintendent wanted to find out more about her new district. She read information and reports, talked to school board members and staff, met with the regional superintendent, and contacted other area superintendents to see if they could provide insight into the school district and its past history and traditions. Based on the information she received and through her review of documents, the superintendent determined that she could provide a needed service to the district by creating a new staff handbook, student schedule, and student handbook.

At a school board meeting during which she showcased her revisions and new creations, some of the school board members were not pleased and in fact were critical of the changes she had made to some of the documents. The superintendent was surprised that the board reacted the way it did because, in her judgment, the changes and the documents themselves were relatively insignificant and did not alter operations or academic requirements.

The superintendent asked the school board for more guidance on these items, but the board could offer nothing substantial. The superintendent contacted a colleague superintendent to review the issue and ask if he had any insight into the board objections. He said that when he was new to his district, he looked for a strategic plan to help him know what the school community and school board valued and what they had been working on in previous years.

She knew that her district did not have a very complete strategic plan. No one had mentioned it as a valued planning document for her to review to gain information about the district.

She brought the idea of developing a new strategic plan to the school board. She told the board that the strategic planning process would result in goals and plans of action to meet identified priority needs in the school district and to strengthen what already is working well. The school board thought this might be something that would help the district and appreciated the effort of the new superintendent to work with the community, the staff, and the school board on collectively setting goals to help serve students.

Advice:

Do not assume that reading reports and talking to a few people provides the rationale necessary to change some things that have existed for years. The school community wants and needs to be involved in change.

Tip: Communicate What's Important

Keeping the focus means having a clear vision of what needs to be accomplished. The question, "What is our mission?" should be asked and answered by the superintendent, administrative team, school board, and members of the school community.

Example:

A retired superintendent decided that two years out of the position was long enough, and he applied for and was hired in a small district. His previous experience was in much larger, more urban school systems. He applied to the small district because he believed he had skills to offer the district and because he had not worked in a small district before and viewed it as a challenge. During his first six months in the district, he met with school board members, administrators, teachers, parents, and community residents. He made a point of visiting the local eating establishments, knowing that many of the retired locals congregated there for morning coffee. He often joined them and talked about the school system, listening carefully to their comments and complaints. He soon discovered that this small community had mixed feelings about their schools (usually dependent upon their school experiences) and that they were not likely to support any increase in taxes to support operational costs or building needs.

The superintendent also learned that most community residents and some employees of the school system held incorrect assumptions regarding student achievement or the quality of education in general. In fact, he found misinformation fairly rampant among many of the residents.

Within about a six-month time period, the new superintendent formulated a plan to improve communication, providing accurate and important school and district information to the community in a variety of ways. He talked to small groups of people wherever he could gain access, including in restaurants, at civic and local government meetings, and before local hospital boards and area planning groups. He developed presentations around three main themes: what is going well in the district (strengths), what is not going well (needs), and what the highest priority issue is that the superintendent and school board should work on in the coming year.

The superintendent also structured school board meetings to include teacher and student presentations that showcased achievement, events, creative projects, and information about each of the schools. The local media were invited to many school events, renewing their interest in covering school-related activities. The superintendent, school board, and media focus on students, their accomplishments, and what was being done to assure student success seemed to turn public perception about the school system around.

One small but important indicator of an improved attitude by parents and others in the community was that open enrollment increased for the first time in five years.

Advice:

Gather information regarding the community perception of the schools and district before embarking on a new strategic planning effort. Strategic plans are district specific, so the more the superintendent knows about his or her district, the more successful the plan will be.

Tip: Don't Let the Planning Process Become the Focus

Keeping the focus on the mission of the organization often means using the strategic plan to identify goals and plans of action to keep the district on track with important initiatives. The planning process helps to assure that the most important issues are identified and that resources are allocated to those priorities. The process is a means to an end; the results of planning are the important part of the process.

Example:

A superintendent, newly hired in a midsized district, was not a great proponent for strategic planning. This superintendent came from a large metropolitan district as an assistant superintendent and had participated in a year-long strategic planning process involving over fifty people and multiple task forces. A consulting firm led the process. The consultants were great facilitators but also very expensive. The end product for the year-long, intensive effort was a bound document identifying three or four goals in six major areas (curriculum, communication, budget, technology, programs and services, and operations). Each of the six task forces was comprised of eight to ten people who developed the goals for their area. It was a five-year plan to be reviewed each year.

There were two events that happened in the second year of the strategic plan implementation: the superintendent left, and the district's operating levy failed to be renewed, so major budget cuts occurred. The fact is the plan was never referred to again. District conditions had changed so much that the planning goals no longer were applicable. The assistant superintendent believed that the planning document was not specific enough to be helpful and that the goals in the plan could have been developed for any large school system because they were too generic. The fact that the plan was not used did not surprise or bother him.

Now, as a new superintendent, he did not want to spend the time, energy, and cost in strategic planning. His new district's goals were obvious to him because the district was rapidly growing and needed two things to happen: keep student achievement levels high and develop and implement plans to accommodate a growing student population.

After supervising multiple building projects, monitoring finances, managing growth, and keeping an eye on student achievement, the superintendent realized that a strategic plan was now needed to refocus energy on the district's educational mission. The superintendent knew it was time to develop a plan focused only on student academic success.

The superintendent wanted to make sure the community and school board were involved in developing a shared vision and mission once the facility, program, and staffing issues were on track for the next several years. Thinking back to the ineffective planning process from his past, the superintendent developed his own, very successful, version of the strategic planning process.

Advice:

How a superintendent maintains the vision and mission of his or her district is as varied as the districts themselves. The best course of action for one system may not be the best for another. Superintendents can and should adjust and modify the planning process as needed to keep the focus on the students.

Tip: Allocate Resources to the Highest Priority Issues

The astute superintendent is involved in the budget development process so that he/she knows how and where resources are distributed. With increasingly limited funds, it is important for the superintendent, with board and community involvement, to determine what those highest priority issues are.

Example:

A rural district had the benefit of a superintendent's leadership for over seventeen years. The superintendent became an institution in the community, and most everyone deferred to the superintendent in all matters of school operation—especially the budget.

The superintendent's leadership style was best described as authoritarian. He conducted the business of the district in a "top down" manner. When the administrators or staff needed money to benefit their area or the students for whom they were responsible, they would have to seek out the superintendent to make a plea for the additional money, staff, or materials. The superintendent would approve, disapprove, or modify the requests. He based his decisions mostly on whose turn it was to "get something." But the superintendent also made judgments on what he believed were important areas for expenditures—or not. He was less likely to approve the sponsorship of a one-act play or yearbook than he was to approve a new chalk machine to mark the football field. He did have some biases.

The students in the district were "adequately" prepared for graduation, with about half attending postsecondary institutions. As the district enrollment slowly declined, it became increasingly obvious that program and personnel cuts were affecting the quality of education in the district. About the time the situation was becoming dire, the superintendent retired. A new superintendent took over the leadership of a district with declining enrollment and a rapidly shrinking budget.

The new superintendent believed that resources should be distributed to fund the district's highest priority needs. He developed a plan of action to help district and community members focus on what they believed to be the most important programs and services for the students in their community. Staff were engaged and involved in identifying what works, what doesn't, and what needed to happen to make sure students had optimal learning opportunities. Once the plan was in place with specific goals and action plans, staff no longer came to the superintendent to plead their case for certain expenditures. They didn't have to because they understood where and why the limited resources were allocated.

This small district survived for a few more years and actually realized some small increase in student achievement scores.

Advice:

In a time of limited resources, it is more important than ever to know what is essential, what is nice to have, and what is unnecessary. Money, time, and personnel are distributed to the greatest needs of the students.

Tip: Focus is Synonymous with Determination

A determination to resolve a problem to everyone's satisfaction can make a difference in the actual solution. Negotiations are difficult under the best of intentions. What can help resolve disputed issues is when the parties involved identify common goals related to the problem. But the parties involved must be determined to try to achieve the best outcome for all concerned.

Example:

A superintendent and his school board decided that the traditional adversarial, position-based bargaining was creating more problems than it solved. The stress level for everyone involved was increasing each bargaining cycle. The decision to move to a calmer, problem-solving approach was met with enthusiasm. What was created was similar to the Interest Based Bargaining Model (IBB) but went well beyond the tenets of IBB by incorporating values held by both union and management leaders. These values included: mutual respect, collaboration, problem solving, and decision making in the best interests of all participants. All parties sought to avoid the cycles of demand and compromise and instead embraced win-win solutions to the problems that confronted the district on a regular basis.

The first problem-solving effort was on the topic of district health insurance costs. The bargaining units involved set up four conditions that they believed were essential to solving the problem of escalating premiums. These four conditions included: provide a comparable health package to what employees already had; reduce or eliminate employee out-of-pocket expenses for health premiums; help the district contain virtually all costs associated with insurance; and help employees become much better consumers of health care.

The problem-solving process started with monthly meetings. Small issues were brought to the table for discussion. The greatest benefit from the monthly meetings was the establishment of trust that, in turn, encouraged open, honest dialogue. Once the members of the groups realized they were in this together sharing a common concern, they became determined to find a win-win solution to the health care premium issue. They educated themselves and sought to find answers to the many questions they and their constituents had about the health issue. They truly did their homework and sought solutions that met all four of the original conditions.

The focus of the group helped lead them to the solutions they believed met their criteria. They communicated the solutions to their members. Each representative of each bargaining group was supportive of the results and, therefore, the issue was a success. Not only were the budgetary concerns met but also the employees became much better consumers of preventative care and they became advocates of seeking ways to further reduce their own health costs.

This superintendent and colleague negotiators found that hard work and determination were important to solve large issues, but they also had to agree on common goals and keep the focus on the desired outcome.

Advice:

Keeping the focus applies to many aspects of leadership. A determination to succeed helps promote resolution to problems that appear to be insurmountable. Identifying common goals that are shared by all involved is a starting point in negotiating positive outcomes.

Chapter Three

Developing an Effective School Board

For a period of time after a superintendent is hired, the relationship between the superintendent and the school board is generally positive. After all, the school board voted (hopefully unanimously) to offer a contract to the person they believe is the best fit for their district. But failure to nurture initial and developing relationships between the superintendent and board members can have negative, long-range consequences. Mistrust, stress, hidden agendas, divided boards, and public disagreements, once started, are very difficult to stop.

Houston and Eadie (2002) believe that "... board-savvy superintendents devote considerable time and attention to building and maintaining a strong, close, and productive working partnership with their boards" (p. 73). The time investment is worth it since poor superintendent–school board relationships can have disastrous effects on the entire educational organization, its mission, and effectiveness. Developing effective school boards is one of the most important responsibilities of a superintendent.

START EARLY

Experienced superintendents encourage those new to the position to work hard on relationship building as soon as they are selected as a finalist. During the interview, the candidate should express his/her core beliefs about education, leadership, governance, and communication. The candidate should also arrive at the interview with some questions for the board about their philosophy, priorities, and expectations for the new superintendent. This initial exchange can assist both parties in determining if there is a common ground upon which to build a future relationship.

The selection process gives both sides the opportunity to assess "goodness of fit." Even with efforts on both sides to learn as much as possible about the expectations and beliefs of each other, there are always some surprises once the contract is signed. But starting early to build relationships helps avoid the feeling of being "duped" by either side once the superintendent starts working in the district.

BE PROACTIVE

There are strategies that can help avert some relationship disasters and set the tone for how relationships develop in the future. These strategies are based on the idea that what is talked about gets attention and what is not talked about does not. The relationship between the superintendent and the board is important and therefore needs to be talked about. The following strategies are helpful in building initial positive and productive relationships.

Meet With Each Board Member Individually as Soon as Possible

Some superintendents schedule breakfast or luncheon meetings with each board member during the time between selection for the position and the actual start date. If that is not possible, then meetings could (or should) be scheduled during the first few weeks on the job. This meeting serves two purposes: to get to know the board member on a more personal level and to determine what the board member believes are the strengths, weaknesses, and highest priorities of the district.

Some superintendents find that it is productive to continue to meet informally with individual board members on a regular basis. If this is done, the superintendent should meet equally with each board member and avoid using the meetings to promote a particular issue.

Develop Operating Principles With the School Board Within the First Two Weeks of Taking the Position

A work-study session is a good format for this meeting. Topics that need discussion and clarification in this session include:

- setting the school board meeting agenda (who, when, how)
- procedures for communication among board members during the meeting
- operational procedures (Robert's Rules, use of Committee of the Whole)
- audience participation (public forum, if, when, how structured)

- board interaction with the audience
- how much the superintendent is expected to speak on issues
- consent agenda items
- preferred format for presentations by staff to the board
- format for developing board materials and how to distribute (email, delivered hard copy)
- use of email and phone messaging by board members and superintendent
- communication with the board on critical matters (emergencies, time-sensitive issues, potential media issues, when they may receive a call from a parent or stakeholder)
- other topics that may be specific to how the board traditionally functions

Establish and Clarify Roles

These roles include: the board as a whole, the directors, officers of the board (especially the board chair), and the superintendent. This discussion could take place at the same work session as the session on operating principles.

An important point to discuss early in the relationship is the chain of command. A new superintendent should clarify how school board members handle calls from the public or from staff. The expectation is that these calls are deferred to the appropriate level in the chain of command—whether to a teacher, principal, or superintendent.

Clarification of roles early on should allow board members and the superintendent to talk safely about expectations: board for the superintendent, superintendent for the board, board for itself, and the superintendent for himself or herself. It is much more difficult to address an out-of-role issue if clarification of roles has not occurred.

COMMUNICATE WELL AND WITH PURPOSE

Encourage Transparency

The information provided to the school board should be accurate, comprehensive, and helpful. Remember that no issue brought to the table for discussion or action is insignificant. The smallest item (i.e., bidding on milk or bread vendors) can escalate to controversy if the information is not complete or accurate.

Board members need enough information on agenda items to feel adequately prepared to discuss or vote on topics brought to their attention. With that in mind, superintendents present both sides of a potentially controversial issue. Experienced superintendents anticipate questions and concerns from the board or the public on these issues. They provide information that addresses those issues before they are brought up at a meeting. If this does not occur, school board members quickly lose trust and confidence in their superintendent if they believe information is withheld or is not thorough.

Develop a Communication Plan

The amount, quality, and content of communication can either build trust or destroy it. How and when the superintendent keeps the board informed is discussed early in the school board and superintendent relationship (as new board members are elected, the operating principles and the communication plan need to be revisited).

The plan should include procedures for communicating issues to the board between meetings. For example, is it acceptable for an individual board member to email an information request to the superintendent? Should that request come through the board chair? Should the superintendent comply but send the information to all board members, not just the one making the request? What about open-meeting law restrictions regarding communication between board meetings? These are the issues that need to be discussed in a communication plan. Remember, all written correspondence between the superintendent and school board, including email, is public and must be made available to the public (or media) if they ask.

Make Recommendations on Action Items

The superintendent is the Chief Executive Officer of the school district charged with making sure the policies established by the school board, as the governing body, are administered and implemented properly. The superintendent is also held accountable for making recommendations to the board that assure the smooth functioning of the organization in the pursuit of its mission. Therefore, on issues requiring school board action, the superintendent should provide accurate, comprehensive, and meaningful information for the board prior to their vote.

Unless an emergency as part of the consent agenda, items requiring a board note should be brought to a school board meeting for discussion before the meeting at which the board takes formal action on the item. Doing this allows the board to request any additional information of the superintendent and ask questions prior to voting. This strategy reduces stress at the board table—especially for the superintendent.

Obviously, some action items do not need a lot of preparation or information, but some do. No matter whether the item is considered important or not, the superintendent makes a recommendation on all action items. Then it is up to the school board to accept, modify, or reject the recommendation. Some feel this is risky for the superintendent's public regard, especially if too many of his/her recommendations are challenged. But it is the job of the superintendent to advocate action that best serves the students and district.

KEEP THE FOCUS

An important responsibility of the superintendent is to help the school board maintain focus on important educational goals. Many school board members do not have a background in school operations, teaching, or leadership. They are laypersons elected to represent the community. For that reason, it is the superintendent's duty to educate the board regarding issues important to the school district and to the mission of the district. Strategic planning helps keep the focus on what is important. This planning process should be tailored to the district and its students. Once the plan is in place, the superintendent keeps the board apprised of progress on strategic goals and action plans.

Many superintendents schedule student and staff presentations as a regular part of every (or every other) school board meeting. This is helpful for the board because they may have little opportunity to stay on top of what is happening in all of the schools—especially in a large system or if they do not have children in the schools. The superintendent can highlight important and successful activities, events, and accomplishments of students and staff during the well-planned, informative presentations.

It is not unusual that the school district community may not know what the school board does. Keeping the focus and reporting progress to the community helps the community know about and be supportive of the work of the superintendent and the school board. The superintendent plays a key role in establishing respect for the board throughout the school district and community.

It is the obligation of the superintendent to make certain that the school district staff and the stakeholders know and understand that the school board is the governing authority in the district. Staff, parents, and other community patrons form opinions about school board roles and its effectiveness from conversations and actions of the superintendent. How the superintendent portrays the school board and individual members ultimately influences how community members and staff view their school system and its quality. The more adept and professional the school board members are portrayed, the more likely they rise to that expectation.

Small actions by the superintendent can foster respect for the school board and its members. Some of these include: introduction of board members at school and district events, school board member information featured on the school district website, and newsletters and official documents sent to the public that include board members' names, offices held, and contact information.

USE COMMON SENSE

Other helpful hints in working with school boards can be classified into a common-sense category.

- The school board should have ample and factual information on agenda items. If at all possible, they should be forewarned and prepared for addressing controversial issues.
- When school board members are prepared, conduct their business professionally, and are focused on their roles and responsibilities, they are more effective as a school board and can govern much more efficiently.
- A school board meeting is a meeting held in the public—not a public meeting. Boards may need occasional gentle reminders of that fact so that they do not become embroiled in arguments with one or more audience members.
- School board members should take advantage of state and national training and orientation sessions.
- The school board chair position is not one that all board members are qualified (or want) to assume.
- The school board should conduct an annual performance review of the superintendent and of themselves as a board using agreed-upon and predetermined criteria.

ESSENCE OF DEVELOPING AN
EFFECTIVE SCHOOL BOARD

School board members should have knowledge of their role as a school board member. Continuous orientation and training helps keep school board members' skills, knowledge, and attitudes as fresh and as helpful as possible to the students, the organization, and the school community. The superintendent is as much a mentor to the school board and its individual members as he/she is to his/her own staff. Training, evaluation of performance, and focus on district priorities helps to define and improve the relationship between the school board and the superintendent. All important relationships take time, energy, and effort to develop, maintain, and grow.

TIPS AND ADVICE

Tip: Help Orient Prospective Board Members

Superintendents and seated school board members may consider developing strategies to help new, prospective board members learn about the role of a school board and how it functions—prior to the filing deadline. Effort should be made to attract "serious" candidates to the school board and to provide a basic understanding of what a school board member does on a governing board.

Example:

In a 3,000 pupil suburban district, school board members were well known. Each of the six members had served at least one four-year term, with the majority serving multiple terms. In the second year of the superintendent's tenure, one of the board members made a decision to not run again (said things were going well so no need to stay to monitor) but did not announce that decision until just two weeks before the filing deadline for November elections. No one from the community filed for the open position.

The vacant seat was filled with the person who had the most write-in votes in the election. That person was a former business manager who had recently retired after thirty years on the job. Name recognition was high for that individual. If the former business manager chose not to take the open seat, then the position would have been offered to the person who had the second most votes and so on. Fortunately for the district, the business manager did take the position and served over ten years as a board member.

This experience, however, brought to the forefront the need to orient the public about the role of the school board and to provide information to prospective candidates. The school board and superintendent determined that offering a thirty-minute question-answer session before a couple of school board meetings would allow interested persons to attend and ask questions regarding school board work. These sessions were held before the filing deadline and occurred immediately before regularly scheduled board meetings (not part of the formal board meeting). The dates and times were published and communicated. The strategy was moderately successful, attracting a few people to the sessions.

Even though attendance was low, the school board believed they provided a service to the community. The wanted to encourage members of the community to consider running for the school board and, at the same time, emphasize the importance of the role of the school board and its responsibility to the district residents.

Advice:

Superintendents should not seek out members of the public to encourage them to run for the school board. This is not good practice. However, school board members can and should talk to individuals believed to have the interest, ability, time, and energy to run for a school board position. Offering opportunities to gain information about the responsibility of being a school board member is a good idea.

Tip: Anticipate Controversial Issues

When anticipating a large and unhappy crowd at a school board meeting, the superintendent and school board chair should meet in advance of the meeting to discuss protocol for the public forum. Topics for this meeting include strategies for addressing public disruptions, disrespectful behavior, nonresidents speaking, and procedures for who can speak, for how long, and on what topics. Being proactive in addressing public behavior at school board meetings helps the board conduct its business with efficiency and decorum.

Example:

A large, suburban district had a long history of public support for authorizing tax increases for building projects and helping with operating costs. A referendum for a continuing operating levy was brought to the public for their vote. Passage of the referendum would not raise taxes but keep them at the current level to continue support for operating costs. In an unanticipated election result, the public voted down the renewal of the levy. The administration and school board thought perhaps that they did not provide enough information to the public about the fact that the approval was critical in order to maintain existing programs and services and that taxes would not increase beyond what people were already paying. So, the issue was brought back to the voters two months later after a more intensive information campaign. The voters defeated the issue at an even greater margin.

The district had already cut about three million dollars from its budget the previous year and now was faced with cutting an additional five million. The time frame for determining and implementing the cuts was about two months. Over 12 percent of the operating budget was cut in eighteen months. This was devastating for the district. The superintendent and administrators began the quick work of identifying potential cuts, looking at programs, staff, services, closing a school, and other items that really amounted to dismantling an efficient, high-achieving, student-centered system. To make matters worse, an organized opposition group began a smear campaign of administrators, teachers, school board members, and the district's financial management.

As budget reductions and cuts were brought to the board table, many members of the public (and the opposition) attended these meetings. Some people created chaos by shouting and vociferously objecting to virtually everything proposed and discussed by the school board. Part of the problem the board faced was that a long-term, very adept school board chair (seventeen years) was defeated in the recent school board elections. The new chair, although also a long-term board member, did not have the same skills in handling controversy, angry people, or inappropriate, disrespectful audience behavior.

The lack of ability of the school board chair to control disruptions caused two events to occur: police were on alert each time the school board met and the opposition gained tremendous notoriety in the media.

The superintendent tried to converse with the board chair about the need to add structure to the meetings. However, even given the chaos, the board chair believed that the public "has the right to speak." Lessons learned from this experience were many: never assume anything in an election; anticipate an organized opposition under the best of circumstances and plan ahead; establish protocol for handling angry or large crowds at school board meetings; and not all school board members have the skills to be a school board chair.

Advice:

A superintendent does not have control over school board members' behavior. But the superintendent can and should help the school board agree on how they want to conduct their business in a public setting. Establishing operating procedures for school board meetings provides stability even in the face of controversy.

Tip: Be Consistent, Follow the Process

There may be times when the relationship between a superintendent and a school board member is strained because of issues affecting the school board member's child who is a student in the district. A superintendent cannot show favoritism toward school board members or to the children of school board members.

Example:

The superintendent and a school board member had a respectful and congenial relationship. In their district, athletics played a prominent role in the schools and community. The district was small enough that many members of varsity teams included sons or daughters of staff or school board members past and present.

Varsity coaches were typically teachers in the district and usually high school staff members. The athletic conference was large enough that students who were very good athletes could end up with scholarships to state universities or colleges, and occasionally Ivy League institutions. As would be expected, some parents believed that their son or daughter deserved more playing time than he/she received. And, if a son or daughter was not given the right opportunities, some parents campaigned for a change in coaching staff.

The superintendent was approached by a school board member who believed that the coach of his son's baseball team was inept and unfair in his treatment of the board member's son. Not enough playing time and not making the varsity team were the two central issues. The board member told the superintendent that his son deserved a chance to prove himself, and due to the lack of skills of the varsity coach, his son was being denied an opportunity to prove just how good he was at his assigned position. The tearful plea eventually came out in the conversation—the coach needs to be fired.

The superintendent listened very carefully to the board member. He asked if the board member had talked to the coach, and the answer was yes. He also reminded the board member about the long-standing policy that playing time was a coaching decision. He asked if the board member talked to the athletic director. The board member said he did but that the athletic director said the coach is experienced and there was no concern that would warrant AD interference with the coach's decisions.

The superintendent asked if the board member could name specific instances that gave substance to the accusation that the coach was inept. The board member relayed that other parents had concerns about the coach, especially since the team did not have a very good winning record. The superintendent reminded the board member that coaches have differing philosophies about participation, about playing seniors, and about skill assessment and development.

The board member was emotional and continued to defend his son against the coach. The superintendent told the board member that firing a coach is not an arbitrary move. Any termination decision requires a process, one that involves observation, evaluation, possible improvement plans, and issues identified by the AD. The superintendent also reminded the board member that superintendent intervention in coaching decisions undermines the AD and his job. It also creates a poor climate among coaching staff since their jobs may hang in the balance depending on who they may offend with playing-time decisions—certainly no way to operate an athletic program. The board member acknowledged, somewhat begrudgingly, that the superintendent is a "process person" and that this situation would be no different than others that he had observed the superintendent handle. The issue of coach termination was not pursued by the board member, but he did have the superintendent's word that complaints from parents and students regarding the athletic program would not be ignored. The superintendent assured the board member that when performance standards were not met for employees, it could result in directives to improve or, when justified, termination.

Advice:

The goal of developing a positive relationship between the superintendent and a school board member is a priority for both parties. This relationship must be based on trust. Trusted superintendents display a consistency of behavior in decision making no matter who is involved—even when the person is a school board member. Listening to concerns—of school board members and the public alike—is as important as the outcome or resolution of a concern.

Tip: Use Expertise of Others

There are times when a superintendent needs to use the services of a neutral facilitator in order to address dissention among board members or issues interfering with the school board–superintendent relationship. Conditions and situations vary as to when this is beneficial, but the astute superintendent knows when circumstances are deteriorating to the point that the relationship with the school board is at risk.

Example:

A newly elected school board member initially appeared to understand her role as a school board member. She also seemed to understand the relationship of individual board members with each other and the superintendent. But, as the months passed, the school board member displayed increasingly "rogue" behavior both at the board table and outside of the board meeting. For example, in one instance before the school board voted on the consent agenda, the newest board member asked the superintendent to explain certain bills. She questioned several bills that were under $100 for food or a payment to a staff member. In many ways, the questioning was justified based on auditor's rules, but in other ways, the time expended at the meeting to explain the payments was becoming disruptive to the meeting. At each subsequent school board meeting, the list of inquiries for specific bills became longer, more detailed, and more negative.

Other agenda items brought for discussion and/or action became "take a stand" issues for the board member. She would not say much during discussion but then would vehemently oppose the recommendation once brought for a vote. Other board members became intimidated by the sporadic and somewhat angry behavior of the new board member. One board member confided in the superintendent that she was concerned that if she questioned the new board member's opinion about something said at the board table, the board member would lash out and publicly humiliate her.

After about eight months, the superintendent met with the board chair and suggested a board retreat on setting board goals and team building. The superintendent knew of a former board member in a large district who now served as a consultant/facilitator for new board members and for school board goal-setting. It was arranged that the facilitator would come to the district and meet with the superintendent and school board to go over key responsibilities of school boards, of individual members, and ways in which the school board and superintendent could function more efficiently and effectively.

The retreat was held, and the facilitator did an excellent job. Every person was able to identify what was working and what he/she would like to change. School board member roles were discussed, as were National School Boards Association standards. The board was encouraged to set goals for their own progress. The new board member realized her questioning and behavior at the board meetings was distracting to other board business. It was suggested that her specific budget questions could be addressed to the superintendent or business official between board meetings as long as the question and response was shared with all board members. Board meetings were much more pleasant after that retreat.

Engaging the services of a neutral facilitator helped the school board and superintendent make progress on identifying concerns and developing strategies to address them.

Advice:

Behavior of just one board member can make every board meeting feel like a punishment. Doing something proactive by involving an outside "expert" can make a difference, especially if the goal of the third-party neutral is clear. A review of school board operating principles is periodically needed. School boards should develop standards for their own effectiveness and evaluate their progress toward those goals.

Tip: Help Board Members Stay in Role

New superintendents—or experienced ones for that matter—ought to avoid direct, public conflict with a board member who attempts to usurp superintendent authority in administrative matters. The exception to the rule is when the board member attacks or demeans others—administrators, teachers, or students. The superintendent should set a meeting with the board member to explain concerns and clarify roles. This meeting may or may not include the school board chair—that is a decision for the superintendent to make.

Example:

In the mid-seventies, the superintendent had a new job in a racially divided district. For the first time, parents who were traditionally "in charge" and had their voices heard loudly and clearly found themselves in the minority. Their champion on the school board was a prominent attorney from a prominent family. He had written the legal brief for the district in trying to forestall desegregation of the school district.

At the first board meeting of the school year, these parents came to the meeting protesting the placement of a particular principal at their children's school on grounds of incompetency. Coincidentally, the principal was one of the best-trained and most successful principals in the district during the previous years of segregation. The board member immediately took the side of the belligerent parents. Since this was a personnel issue, the superintendent suggested to the board chairperson that the parents make their comments at the end of the school board meeting during a time reserved for public input. He further suggested that any discussion of the principal's qualifications be conducted in executive session after the meeting.

By the end of the meeting, the parents, now calmer, were able to make a concise expression of their dissatisfactions. In the executive session, the aggressive board member was able to function more as a school board member rather than a public defender. The principal's record and accomplishments satisfied the board that the competency of the principal was not an issue. The board concluded that the parents' distress primarily stemmed from dislocation out of their previous school. The administration recommended that the principal host several parent meetings in the fall to enhance parent adjustment to their new situation. Parents were invited to regularly visit the school and, with principal and teacher approval, schedule time in classrooms if they wanted to observe or help.

The day after the board meeting, the superintendent invited the attorney/board member to meet with him. At the meeting, the superintendent explained how the unannounced demonstration was unfair to all concerned. The board member could not unilaterally work with groups against the board and administration. The superintendent said that the board member should bring matters affecting the administration of the schools to the superintendent first, giving the superintendent a chance to solve the problem. He also said that personnel matters should be discussed in executive session before they are brought to the board as a whole. There was never a need for another such meeting between this board member and the superintendent.

Advice:

A group of angry or upset parents can create a great amount of tension at a school board meeting. It is sometimes a challenge for the board members to maintain a calm demeanor and to follow proper protocol for how and when the public can address the school board. The board conducts its business in the public, but it is not a public meeting—keeping that in mind is helpful.

Chapter Four

Building an Administrative Team

One of the most daunting challenges facing a first-time superintendent is the adjustment to a new role. And, for many new superintendents, they must simultaneously adjust to an unfamiliar organization and school community. This transition must be done quickly, seamlessly, and effectively. Most administrators new to their position hope for a "honeymoon period" to allow them to make this adjustment. Unfortunately, the Chief Executive Officer of the organization is seldom provided a honeymoon time period and, if there is one, it is very short. So, when the first complex issue makes its way to the superintendent's desk, whether a day into his/her tenure or a month, the expectation is that she/he resolves the issue effectively and efficiently.

It is eminently better to come into a new position forewarned and forearmed with the knowledge that precious little time is accorded the superintendent to prepare for the onslaught of issues. As quickly as possible, even before officially on board, a major priority task for the new CEO is the formation of the superintendent's cabinet, executive council, or administrative team.

SELECT THE ADMINISTRATIVE TEAM MEMBERS

The administrative team is the cadre of subordinate administrators who work closely with the superintendent to orchestrate the effective and efficient operation of the organization. The team keeps the superintendent apprised of critical events, data, and developments that may affect the quality of his/her decision making and problem solving. Team members who are loyal, knowledgeable, organizationally astute, and respected leaders in their own right allow the superintendent to focus on the mission, vision, and goals of the organization. A high-functioning, empowered administrative team assists the superintendent in his or her ability to function much more effectively in his/her role.

The superintendent has the latitude to chose who he/she wants on the administrative team. Typically, team members are administrators already assigned major roles in the school districts' chain of command. Human resources, curriculum and instruction, business, community relations, operations, and special programs are often members of the team, particularly if their titles include assistant/associate superintendent, director, supervisor, or coordinator. Smaller school district's administrative team—with flatter organizational charts—may be comprised of only the building principals.

Depending on the size and complexity of the organization, administrative teams range in number from five to ten members. Team members are virtually always responsible for oversight and management of a major strand of the organization. Additionally, the members are directly subordinate to the superintendent and have equal "power ranking" with each other. This is important for open dialogue with the superintendent and among members themselves—no fear of retribution.

UNDERSTAND THE PURPOSE
OF ADMINISTRATIVE TEAM MEETINGS

The new superintendent has the latitude to schedule administrative team meetings as often as he/she sees fit in order to realize the greatest advantage the team can provide. Understanding the purpose of the meetings leads to greater efficiency. Administrative team meetings should:

- Keep the superintendent informed of organizational developments, data, events, and emerging issues
- Apprise administrative team members and the superintendent of developments in each major area of the organization
- Facilitate collaboration across departments and organizational areas in resource use and program development
- Enhance camaraderie
- Strengthen inter- and intradepartmental communication
- Allow for discussion, deliberation, and resolution of complex problems
- Facilitate decision making
- Promote planning and strategizing
- Assist in preparing for meetings of the school board, including setting meeting agendas

The new superintendent should use the administrative team to become familiar with the district's past practices, polices, strengths, priorities, needs/weaknesses, organizational relationships, and other issues important to understanding the school district and community. The adept superintendent can fast-track his/her learning curve simply by asking of, listening to, and questioning members of the administrative team.

Another, and perhaps one of the most important purposes of the administrative team meeting, is the delegation of tasks. The superintendent uses the meeting and agenda items to ask team members to gather data, report on specific actions, create task forces or committee structures, convene/attend meetings, prepare reports, and perform other duties as needed. The superintendent must weigh these delegated duties against the existing workloads of the team members.

PLAN FOR FREQUENT MEETINGS

There is nothing more important in the work lives of administrative team members than contributing to the success of the superintendent in leading and guiding the school district. Given that fact, the frequency and duration of administrative team meetings is dependent on the time needs of the superintendent. The question to ask is, "What amount of time is needed for the superintendent to understand the organization's complexities and to develop quality decisions?"

Most superintendents find that complex organizations require regularly scheduled weekly meetings of at least two hours. Less complex organizations may find that less meeting time is needed, but virtually all organizations benefit from weekly meetings. Infrequent meetings between the superintendent and the administrative team suggests a lack of focus on and limited communication about critical district issues.

The meeting frequency is also dependent on what the superintendent thinks the purpose of the meeting is and what contribution the meeting can make to the work of the organization. In other words, the administrative team meetings are well planned, meaningful, and result in one or more accomplishments focused on organizational improvement, management, planning, data analysis, and/or reporting. Drucker (2006) said that the effective executive "states at the outset of a meeting the specific purpose and contribution it is to achieve. He makes sure the meeting addresses itself to this purpose" (p. 69). Superintendents operate their administrative meetings with regularity and purpose.

An important point is that some superintendents or subordinate administrators may believe that frequent, one-on-one meetings produce the same valuable result as a coordinated administrative meeting. This is not the case. Disjointed delegation and planning cannot benefit the district and its school community nearly as much as coordinated, collaborative team efforts focused on district plans and goals.

PREPARE FORMAL AGENDAS

Administrative team meetings, because they serve such an important function, are agenda driven. Formal written agendas should be prepared in advance of the meetings. Team members are encouraged to contribute items to the agenda and to be prepared to address those items in the meeting.

Typically agenda items are organized by function: meeting dates/times; discussion items; action items; correspondence; and other. Action items are usually the highest priority items on the agenda and are arranged early in the meeting time. A helpful strategy is to allocate a designated amount of time for each item—keeping the agenda moving and productive.

Among the agenda structure, one item is of particular assistance to the superintendent because it provides information of which the superintendent may not otherwise be aware. This item is department or individual member reports about his/her areas of responsibility. The members use this time to share major initiatives, trouble spots, improvements, and successes. The sharing of significant department information provides the opportunity for all members and the superintendent to understand the complexities of the entire organization, foster mutual respect, enhance teamwork, and encourage open communication. This activity also gives the superintendent possible items to place on the school board agenda as a report of information.

ENCOURAGE THE TEAM MODEL

Administrative team meetings provide a quality model for team members to use in their own departments. They can use the team model to structure meetings with their lead staff. Furthermore, any number of agenda items from the administrative team meeting can be placed on the department meeting agenda. This practice enhances communication across the organizational strands and keeps staff informed, and even involved, in important decisions that affect the entire school system.

Throughout the span of the school district's organizational chart and at all levels, the administrative team model reinforces important principles of quality leadership/management. Remember, the team meeting structure is not just for the purpose of disseminating information and solving problems. It also provides opportunities to building connections throughout the organization (Kouzes and Posner, 2002).

DEVELOP THE TEAM MEMBERS

The administrative team is both a work group and a planning group. The skills needed by the team members to function effectively with the superintendent are referenced briefly in the above paragraphs. To be more specific, the team members are expected to be quality administrators, effective leaders, respected decision makers, and excellent communicators.

In order for the administrative team to be successful, individual team members must fulfill the responsibilities of his or her job but also be a valued contributor to the administrative team meetings. Not all members of the team know about team building, collaboration, professional learning communities, proactive leadership, strategic planning processes, or other team or leader concepts. In those instances, the superintendent provides professional development opportunities for the team or for individual members. Developing team members leads to developing an excellent team. The qualities associated with team excellence often include: clear goals; results-driven structure; competent team members; unified commitment; collaborative climate; standards of excellence; external support; and principled leadership (Larson and LaFasto, 1989). To achieve results from the work of the administrative team, the superintendent spends time on team-member development through specialized professional development opportunities and through an important but sometimes overlooked activity, mentorship.

ESSENCE OF BUILDING AN ADMINISTRATIVE TEAM

New superintendents face staggering challenges in leading complex educational systems in the twenty-first century. While it is "lonely at the top," the school CEO need not be alone in fulfilling the duties and responsibilities of the position. A well-designed, high-functioning administrative team offers great promise in providing a jump start into quality leadership before the "honeymoon period" is over.

TIPS AND ADVICE

Tip: Team Behavior Starts With the Superintendent

The superintendent has the ability to create a competitive administrative team or a collaborative administrative team. The expectations she or he sets for individual team member interaction determine the tenor of the group and how the group functions as a team.

Example:

A new superintendent was pleasantly surprised to find that the district's administrative team was a cohesive, respectful, well-functioning group of educators. The administrative team in this district consisted of ten building principals who met weekly with the superintendent. The cabinet was another group who met weekly as well and consisted of the director level administrators: business, curriculum, personnel, community education, special education, and operations. Once a month both groups met together.

This was not a familiar system to the new superintendent, but she believed that its structure was effective—at least from what she could determine in talking with each of the administrators. To enhance her familiarity with the group function and topics of discussion, the new superintendent read minutes of the past year's meetings. It became clear to her that the administrative meetings, those with the principals, were opportunities to talk about and plan in three major categories: building goals and activities, district mission/goals, and concerns or issues. Other topics were mentioned, but each week the three themes were always discussed.

The new superintendent decided to keep the typical administrative team agenda for a while so she could have a greater sense of how the team functioned. She also used the time to gain insight into team members' skills, their interaction, topics of discussion, and overall goal progress.

After about six months, the new superintendent kept the administrative team structure and much of the agenda style from the previous superintendent. She saw the administrative team as a cohesive, well-functioning group. The most impressive quality of the team was its support of each other. They not only supported each other as administrators but they also took pride in successes at each other's schools. Whether things were going well or when a team member faced a particular challenge in his or her building, other team members were there if needed.

This teamwork did not happen overnight. The previous superintendent had nurtured the team concept by encouraging respect, setting a positive tone for the team and the district, and by maintaining a focused agenda each week so each administrator could "brag," lament a problem, share a concern or a new idea, and network with colleagues—all in a safe meeting environment. The new superintendent knew she would have to work hard to improve upon something that was working very well. She also knew that it was her responsibility to make sure the culture of the group remained as supportive and goal-oriented as possible.

Advice:

New superintendents do not need to undo and redo everything from the previous administration. Be astute enough to recognize when something is working well and when to leave certain organizational structures alone.

Tip: Trust Others to Do Their Jobs

Hiring the best administrators is a high priority for a successful superintendent. The hiring process includes recruiting, selecting, supporting, mentoring, and supervising. Once hired, administrators should have the latitude to do their job and make decisions specific to their assigned area of responsibility. Empowered administrators take accountability and responsibility more seriously than administrators who are micromanaged.

Example:

The superintendent of a 6,000-pupil school district made personnel his highest priority. He valued the hiring process for all employees and emphasized to the school board and the principals the need to hire the best possible candidate for every job. The superintendent also believed that once hired, employees should be encouraged, mentored, and supported in their work and in their own professional development. His administrative team provided the vehicle for him to discuss the district's vision, mission, operations, problems, and most importantly, for him to provide mentorship.

The superintendent was supportive of his administrators and provided opportunities for them to grow professionally to gain increased confidence in their leadership skills. For example, the superintendent encouraged district- and building-level administrators to participate in doctorate programs if they did not already have their PhD or EdD. The superintendent was able to solicit both time (release time to attend classes if needed) and resources (tuition reimbursement) for administrators enrolling in doctoral-level education programs. During his tenure, the superintendent saw five administrators (principals and assistant principals) earn their doctorate and five more enroll in a doctoral program.

Because of the care, concern, and mentoring shown to administrators by the superintendent, the administrators also adopted a similar approach to their staff. They followed hiring policies to a tee and had each teacher candidate demonstrate lessons to select parents, teachers, students, and staff. They followed up with multiple reference checks for candidates considered for hiring. This emphasis on personnel—hiring, mentoring, and empowering—proved to be a valuable asset to the district and to student achievement. The superintendent, in his way, built an administrative team that felt valued, involved, and supported in their work. This made each administrator strive to do his or her best and to rise to high expectations for his or her job performance.

Advice:

The nurturing of the administrative team provides the superintendent with a qualified, capable group of administrators who do their job and do it well. This support network builds relationships and develops a synergy in the district that encourages every person to do his or her best to serve students.

Tip: Seek First to Understand

It is important to know how each administrative team member views new educational goals or initiatives before the implementation phase is started. Sometimes the superintendent should ask each team member what he/she thinks before moving forward. Not every team member may be comfortable speaking up, but if the opportunity is provided, it is more likely to happen. The superintendent should demonstrate that he/she is open to dissenting voices or to differing opinions.

Example:

The superintendent in a suburban district was a leader who valued standards-based instruction. Her previous professional experience led her to strongly believe in the standards-driven instruction model. In her district, she had taken a very clear and public stance advocating the use of standards to drive instruction. The strategic plan for the district included specific reference to this initiative. A consulting firm was hired to assure professional development for staff who would be involved in the plan. The administrative team was in the beginning stages of designing the formal plan for implementation.

During one particular meeting with the administrative team, the superintendent gave an overview of standards-driven instruction, setting the context for the remainder of the meeting. After she was finished presenting the information, she asked if there were any questions and whether everyone was in agreement with the overview. One team member responded that he did not really understand standards and was questioning whether all of the principals did either. Then the person asked, "Are we really ready to do this?" There was an awkward silence, and then the superintendent responded by saying, "That is a great question." She asked each team member to share with the group his/her understanding of what standards-driven instruction meant to them. It became apparent that not everyone was in agreement with what they thought it was or how it would be implemented in the schools.

The superintendent spent a significant amount of time over the next several months making sure the administrative team members had a clear and shared understanding of standards and how they serve as a driver for significantly changing school and classroom practices. As a result, the design and final presentation of the plan was coherent, coordinated, and successful.

Advice:

If a climate of trust does not exist among team members, critical information may be withheld or altered so that the superintendent is not aware of questions, concerns, or disagreements. If this happens, full and successful implementation of new ideas is unlikely.

Tip: It is Hard to Change the "Fabric" of a Person

A new superintendent may have to work very hard at building an administrative team if there has not been a formal structure for such a concept before. The administrative team does not just happen without preparation and discussion of what it is and how it works.

Example:

A new superintendent had been part of a large district that had a well-functioning administrative team. When he arrived in the smaller district, he found that there was no administrative team at all and in fact, the six principals, two central office directors, three central office coordinators, and four assistant principals did not have any formal communication with the previous superintendent other than occasional meetings called about issues that emerged as important at the time. The superintendent immediately set up a weekly meeting schedule with a newly formed executive council (principals, business manager, and curriculum director) and set up monthly administrative team meetings (all building level and central office administrators).

The superintendent found that the executive council meetings began to function well rather quickly after he explained the purpose of the meetings, set clear agendas, followed up with meeting minutes, and asked for any additional items from the team each week. The administrative team meetings did not proceed as well. In those meetings, his agenda provided for roundtable discussions, team-building activities, celebration of special events, and end-of-the-year retreats to debrief about the year and set goals for the next year.

After a couple of years, the superintendent did not have the feeling that the administrative team meetings were going as well as they should or could. He tried changing the dates and times of the meetings (asking the group what they preferred), and he altered the agendas so some items were put in writing (housekeeping kinds of updates and information) and encouraged more interaction at the meetings on planning issues.

On the surface, the superintendent believed that the meetings met the goal of keeping team members apprised of what other administrators were doing and what important issues faced the district. The aspect of the meeting that was not going well was the personal interaction—especially between two team members. Although subtle, it was becoming more like the "elephant in the room." The superintendent did talk to each member individually about how this situation impacted the administrative group and its cohesiveness. Each agreed to work on making the situation less tense.

The administrative team never really did mesh the way the superintendent would have liked. Sometimes a change in the team members is necessary. It may be the superintendent who has to be the one to suggest to an administrative team member that it is time to move on, to find a district that is a better match with the administrator's beliefs, skills, and disposition.

Advice:

The formation of an administrative group is important. A well-functioning group has purpose, direction, and a sense of accomplishment. When one or more members of a team are not team players, the effectiveness of the team is compromised. Not even the best leader can make someone be an effective team member.

Tip: Confidentiality is Critical

Administrative team members are privy to information that is confidential. The loyalty of the team is critical for the administrative team to function effectively. Administrators have position power, and any administrator who seeks more power than given by his/her position has the potential to be a rogue administrator by using district information as a way to gain additional recognition/power. Information is power, as the saying goes. Astute superintendents are aware of this and modify the administrative team meetings to limit the impact of confidentiality breaches.

Example:

Each administrative team meeting had a specific agenda. The superintendent used the meetings to stay up-to-date with department and building issues and to monitor progress on the highest priority goals for the district. The administrators were supportive of the goals and the direction the district was taking regarding improved student achievement. The relatively new superintendent was facing significant budget reductions over the next two years and naturally that topic was one of importance during the administrative meetings.

The team was comprised of seven building principals and the directors of business, curriculum, and special education. The meetings were held once per week. The administrative group was a mixture of long-term and relatively new administrators. One of the principals was a twenty-five-year veteran who had a reputation of being the "go to" person for most of the district. The administrator did not apply for the superintendent opening two years ago even though many in the school district community thought he might do so. But he did like the attention from staff and parents about the possibility of applying for the position.

The new superintendent sensed a quiet competition with the principal but was fairly comfortable with the relationship established over the first two years of his tenure.

The administrative team agenda included upcoming budget reductions. There was some evidence presented that would indicate the closing of one or more of the district's elementary schools was an option to consider. Although in initial stages of discussion, the topic was on the administrative team agenda for two weeks in a row.

Soon after the meeting, the superintendent received a call from a community member who lived in the neighborhood where one of the small schools considered for closing was located. The community member was upset and accused the superintendent of secretly planning to close the school without telling the community. She said that she and others would attend the next school board meeting to protest the closing of their school. The superintendent talked for an hour with the person and let her know that all options were on the table for serious budget reduction considerations. He did not avoid the issue, but he indicated that discussions were just starting and that it would be some time before recommendations were made to present to the school board. He also affirmed that closing a school requires a public hearing, so there would be opportunity for community input if that ever became the decision.

This seemed to placate the community member, but the superintendent knew that the "peace" would be short-lived.

The issue facing the superintendent was whether or not he could trust all members of his administrative team. He did not want to bring up the topic of a breach in confidentiality with the administrative team because he did not know for sure that was the case. But the superintendent became more guarded in the future when sensitive budget items were brought to the team for discussion.

Advice:

There is probably nothing as discouraging for a superintendent as the lack of confidentiality of his or her administrative team. There really is not a good solution to that problem. Limiting information or changing team structure is one option.

Chapter Five

Enhancing School-Community Relations

School board members frequently identify "excellent communication skills" as a desired quality of a prospective superintendent candidate. School board members know that the public image of their district often rests on how well their superintendent communicates with both "internal" and "external" clients. Whether speaking, writing, presenting, listening, or using technology, superintendents build and influence an impression about the quality of the educational system they represent. Even in the most informal contact with a stakeholder, the superintendent has to think about how and what is communicated.

Communication with the public is not just about image. School reform efforts, to be successful, must include support from the community. This support extends beyond the organization's internal efforts in team building and development of a shared vision (Jazzar and Algozzine, 2006). Enhancing school-community relations is not only desirable but also necessary for the district to move forward in successfully meeting goals affecting student achievement.

EMBRACE COMMUNICATION RESPONSIBILITIES

Ability to communicate well is expected of all superintendents. While day-to-day communication consumes a majority of the superintendent's time, other communication responsibilities are broader in scope but are no less time-consuming. These include:

- Serving as the district spokesperson to the media.
- Delivering comments (speeches) at public events.

- Providing information to staff, parents, and the community regarding district finances, student achievement, crisis situations, traditions, new initiatives, and overall goals of the district.
- Sharing relevant/critical issues with staff, students, parents, and the community.
- Marketing the district to prospective families.
- Meeting with political representatives to discuss resources, policies, and legal issues.
- Reporting educational progress to local and state supervisory agencies.
- Building partnerships with other educational organizations.
- Providing opportunities for staff and stakeholders to participate in school planning.
- Maintaining close communication with the school board regarding district needs, issues, and decisions.

Although not a finite list, the importance of any one of these communication responsibilities cannot be minimized. Experienced superintendents embrace this responsibility and opportunity to inform, connect, and showcase their district, students, staff, school board, and community.

APPLY COMMUNICATION RULES

Experienced school leaders know there are certain "rules" to follow regarding communication effectiveness. Some of these are:

1. Be genuine, honest, and factual.
2. Know your subject well before you speak. Be prepared.
3. Admit when more study or information is needed to respond to questions, comments, or concerns.
4. Research controversial topics before meeting with small or large groups of people. Anticipate the questions that may be asked—including the most negative and challenging ones. Think about a response. Better yet, address the answers to anticipated questions in preparatory remarks or in the presentation itself.
5. Use email as a good, quick way to send or receive information but not to conduct extensive conversations, handle troublesome issues, or conduct personnel business.
6. Always check spelling and grammar in written communication. Have at least one other person read important communications to staff or the community at large.

7. Introduce school board members at events.
8. When invited to speak at a school event, remember to recognize the building principal and those responsible for organizing the event.
9. Think about the audience to whom you are speaking or writing. Parents and/or community members may not appreciate complicated, long, educational rhetoric. The message may be lost in the delivery.
10. Keep the school board informed on important district issues—before they hear about it from a staff or community member.
11. Keep principals and administrative team members informed of issues affecting their area of supervision before they hear about it from staff or parents.
12. Be aware that nonlicensed personnel are part of the information loop.
13. Write down comments when interviewing with the media—if there is time.
14. Be proactive in addressing issues that could generate negative publicity.
15. Avoid getting into battles with or in the media. Engaging in banter through letters to the editor or blogs casts a negative light on all participants.
16. Always be professional and thoughtful even when others are not.

Communication "rules" are helpful, but superintendents understand that most of what they say is repeated, and probably not with a great deal of accuracy. The listener and even the media may repeat/report "out-of-context" phrases. On the other hand, if too much caution is used in conversation and communication for fear of being misquoted, a superintendent begins to sound like a bureaucrat, projecting an insincere or aloof demeanor.

It is helpful to understand that even informal conversations with staff, parents, community members, or school board members hold potential for spawning rumors, misinterpretations, and misinformation. Few people in the public eye always avoid making communication missteps. Sometimes it is worth correcting the mistake, but often the lesson is to focus on future communication opportunities.

COMMUNICATE WITH A VARIETY OF AUDIENCES

Communicating with community members, parents, staff, and students is time-consuming but necessary. Pride in local schools unites a community and provides a support network for local education initiatives. Trusted school leaders shape public opinion about the organization. They often are responsible for garnering acceptance and allegiance of those in the school community.

They communicate important information, student progress, program and school improvements, and future direction to the larger school community. Razik and Swanson (2010) state that "just as clarity, credibility, and directionality are influenced by organizational changes, an administrator's clear perception of the organization and the power of communication as a shaping agent must constantly sharpen" (p. 138).

Community

The superintendent uses a variety of ideas and methods to engage the community in school operation and mission. These may include:

- District newsletters
- Websites
- Focus groups
- Community education programs
- Business partnerships
- Collaborative activities
- Planned media coverage
- Student community service
- Surveys
- Community celebrations
- Personal invitations to school events/performances
- Tours of schools
- Community representation on specific school or district committees
- Concerted efforts to communicate with hard-to-reach community members

As would be expected, community connections are enhanced by involvement of the superintendent in community activities. Participating on charitable boards and in civic organizations, volunteering for community service, meeting with local clergy, speaking at city council and chamber events, hosting legislative forums, shopping at local businesses, and attending community events are all part of the important responsibilities of the superintendent.

Parents

Superintendents also know that without parent involvement and support, very little progress can be made to improve opportunities for all students. Sergiovanni (1999) said, "When teachers, students and parents are connected to the same ideas, they become connected to each other as well" (p. 112). A strong home-school connection leads to increased opportunities for student success.

Communicating with parents is a primary responsibility of teachers and principals. However, superintendents can provide some meaningful opportunities for parent involvement. Too often superintendents may find that they only interact with parents when difficult issues find their way to the superintendent's desk. Some strategies a superintendent can use to maintain positive parent connections include:

- Attend parent organization meetings (usually by invitation or on a scheduled basis)
- Identify opportunities for parents to be involved on district committees, task forces, or focus groups
- Conduct parent satisfaction surveys
- Encourage parent and volunteer appreciation events
- Be visible in the community
- Recognize, publicly, the importance of parent involvement in schools and with their children
- Respond in a timely fashion to parent calls or questions
- Promote the chain of command so parents can be assured that their issues are heard and by the person who is closest to the issue
- Avoid "going around" the principal in communicating with parents from his/her building

Staff

The superintendent relies on staff to provide excellent programs and services. Communication with staff is essential to enhance and maintain morale and a positive, productive school climate. District size often determines how easily the superintendent can communicate with all staff. The larger the district, the more difficult it is for a superintendent to have personal contact with each staff member. However, several communication strategies can apply to most districts. These are:

1. Welcome staff back to school at the beginning of the year. This activity can set the tone for the year, identify priorities, clarify direction and goals, and provide a positive message of encouragement and appreciation. Drucker (1999) encouraged the organization's leadership to involve and inform the staff about the organization's mission. Not only do the employees need to know about the mission but also they need to believe

in it. Speaking to all staff at a beginning-of-the-year meeting is a great opportunity to refresh the mission of the organization and to identify the highest priority goals for the year.

2. Stop by classrooms to greet staff and students. Always check in the office first and let the principal know you are in the building and why.
3. Take time to visit with the custodial, food service, and office staff. Keep them informed of and included in district initiatives and major decisions.
4. Speak to building staff once or twice a year. Provide an update of district work and recognize special activities conducted by the staff. Allow time for questions. Again, this should be scheduled with the building principal.
5. Recognize that nonlicensed staff can feel out of the loop. Special effort to keep them informed is worth the time investment. Razik and Swanson (2010) speak to the idea of message directionality. Their thought is that as information moves through a system (usually top down) the message is increasingly filtered. This can further exacerbate the feeling of subordinate staff that they, indeed, are not part of the larger system if they receive information last or receive information that is incomplete.

Students

A challenge for the superintendent is to find meaningful strategies to enhance communication with students. The presence of a superintendent in a school building may not produce any positive interaction with students unless students have had some previous contact or knowledge of who the superintendent is and what he/she does. Connecting with students requires deliberate planning. Some strategies for enhancing communication with students include:

- Conducting exit interviews with a random sampling of seniors
- Serving as a guest speaker or reader in a classroom
- Attending a variety of school functions
- Stopping by classrooms to say hello (with the teacher's prior knowledge if possible)
- Scheduling five to ten minutes of interaction with students at existing student clubs and organizations
- Serving as a judge for competitions
- Eating lunch in the student lunchroom (with students)
- Volunteering to help with student-organized events
- Serving food in the lunch line
- Volunteering to teach a class for a period or day
- Serving as a bus monitor
- Sending personal, handwritten congratulatory letters to students on their accomplishments

- Including students on task forces or district committees
- Recognizing student achievement in newsletters
- Conducting high school follow-up surveys
- Conducting student focus groups on specific topics of interest to the students
- Attending events at alternative schools and adult education programs

Students can provide information to the superintendent about their school experiences. They are willing to rise to the occasion if asked. Effective superintendent interactions with students are meaningful, short, and friendly.

ESSENCE OF ENHANCING
SCHOOL-COMMUNITY RELATIONS

Superintendents who speak from the heart, use a variety of vehicles for communications, think about what their audience wants to know, and treat everyone with respect and dignity are successful in promoting the district to its stakeholders. Communication is not just writing, speaking, and listening. Body language and nonverbal responses carry as much influence as words, written or spoken. The superintendent is the district representative and designated leader—someone others look to for guidance, information, and direction. Communication provides an opportunity to advocate for the students and for the mission of the school system.

TIPS AND ADVICE

Tip: Know When to Be Flexible

Sometimes a superintendent has to make a decision that will disappoint students—it is unavoidable. The best that can be done is to keep the best interests of the entire school community in mind. However, there are situations that may lead a superintendent to rethink the original decision and subsequently, modify his or her position. There is nothing wrong with modifying a position if it is determined that it ultimately creates the least disruption to the students and the school community.

Example:

A high school principal informed the superintendent in early September about a concern regarding the play chosen for fall production. The superintendent met with the principal, activities director, and play director to briefly discuss the production. He left the decision with those entrusted with play selection and approval. Several days after the meeting, the superintendent received a couple of calls from concerned parents of students who had already been chosen for roles in the play. The parents believed the play "stepped over the line" with a violent theme (even though it was a musical, its theme was about killing people to be baked in pies).

The superintendent contacted the principal and asked a few more questions about the play. It was soon revealed that the play director was happy with the play selection (rehearsals had started) but said that it probably should not be shown to students under the age of twelve. This fact was not mentioned in the initial discussions.

The first reaction of the superintendent was to shut down production, believing that the family-friendly nature of all plays traditionally presented by the high school had been greatly compromised. Once his decision became known, other parents of students who had roles in the play called the superintendent to complain that it wasn't fair to their child to stop the play at this point. It was too late to select another play, so the result would be "no fall play."

The school board was kept informed as soon as the first parent calls were received. The superintendent anticipated that this could end up being an issue brought to the school board for a decision since two groups of parents held such differing points of view regarding the superintendent's decision. The superintendent did not think that the board should be placed in the position of having to overturn the administration's decision to cancel the play or, on the other hand, be faced with an entire high-school-student contingent who would no doubt protest the cancelling of the play if the board supported the administration's decision.

The superintendent quickly formed a task force to hear both sides. The task force was comprised of two parents, an elementary principal, a mayor, and two board members. The group heard "testimony" from the play director and from the superintendent. The superintendent's position was that high school plays have always been for the school community at large. Elementary and middle school students were bused to the high school to have their own viewing. Plus, senior citizens always came out in large numbers to see the plays.

The director said it was a high school version of the play, so it was modified from the adult version and should be fine for high school performance even though younger students may not appreciate the content.

The committee voted three to three to stop the play—in effect, a stalemate. Because of that task force outcome, the superintendent then modified his original decision to cancel the play and allowed the play to continue. But he imposed conditions: all posters and advertisements about the play would clearly state it was not appropriate for children under twelve; the student activity policy would be revised to reflect the fact that all play proposals would need to be approved four months in advance; at least two plays would be offered for approval in case a backup one is needed; and that all performances would be for general audiences unless otherwise approved as an exception. The play did go on, and no further controversy resulted. The policy review and revision prevented this issue from reoccurring.

Advice:

Sometimes a decision is initially made for the right reason, but additional circumstances and information may cause a modification to that decision. It is often wise to involve a small group of neutral people in controversial issues so they can review information in an unbiased manner.

Tip: Meet the Public on Their Turf

Communicating with the public is not just about hosting public forums or asking the public to attend meetings in the schools. Sometimes it is better (and wiser) to go to the public with important messages. A superintendent who goes out of his or her way to connect with the public sends a strong message that he/she recognizes how hard it is for some patrons to leave work, find sitters, or interrupt their lives to go to a meeting about school business.

Example:

In a rapidly growing school district, construction of new schools seemed to occupy the superintendent's agenda for a six-year time span. When the superintendent was hired, it was with the knowledge that a new school would be needed in two years or even sooner if the growth continued at the same rate (or greater) as in the past three years. A bond referendum was passed allowing for a fast-track school construction process to help relieve some of the space pressures. The superintendent knew that the growth pattern showed no immediate sign of slowing, so she let the public know that in a few years, another school may be needed. The community was primarily a bedroom community of a larger urban center. There were, however, two factories in the district that each employed about 350 workers. Many of the workers lived in the district, but about half did not. When a second bond referendum was presented four years later for building another new school, the superintendent believed it was very important to seek ways to reach out to the community about the need for the school.

Even though it would be six years from the time the first building was built and when the second would open, the superintendent knew the public would feel like it was "just yesterday" that the district had asked them for money to build a school. With few local business and commercial property, the burden of construction costs really rested with homeowners.

The superintendent knew she needed to be accessible to as many residents as possible to explain the need and the tax impact. She contacted the two factories located in the district and spoke to the plant managers. She explained that she would greatly appreciate an opportunity to make herself available to workers between each of the three shifts. She received permission to advertise within the factory her availability to the workers between shifts to discuss the upcoming vote and to answer questions. The shifts for each factory started at 7 A.M., 3 P.M., and 11 P.M. A few workers took advantage of the time and visited with her about the need for the school, the tax impact, and the school district in general.

The end result was that the attendance at her information sessions was not that great, but the public relations was. Word quickly spread that the superintendent took the time to be at the factories to meet with the workers—on their time schedule. No one from the schools had ever been to their place of work before to talk to them. This activity, along with many other planned events and presentations, helped to pass the referendum. An operating levy presented to the voters at the same time in a separate ballot question also passed.

Advice:

Enhancing school-community relations takes planning. Part of this plan must include reaching out to various community groups. Going to where the people are instead of always expecting the public to come to the schools for meetings produces benefits. Meeting with the public on their turf produces good public relations. But more than that, it may also provide insight into the pulse of the community. A final but very important point is, don't just go to the public when something is needed from them. Communication about schools is an ongoing, continuous process.

Tip: Communicate, Communicate, and When in Doubt, Communicate More

Successful superintendents understand the need to proactively communicate with all stakeholder groups. Communication should be focused, honest, and geared toward the intended audience. This approach builds trust and helps to move the entire school system vision forward.

Example:

In a midsize rural district with 17,000 students, there are several local and online newspapers that provide regular coverage of all school-related events.

The community is tight knit, and there is a vested interest in the success of the school system. Discussions about school system activities are pervasive. When the superintendent was hired in the district, there was no defined communication plan—either formal or informal. Most communication to the public was in response to something that happened—reactive rather than proactive.

In collaboration with others in the district, the superintendent established a communication plan. The plan included strategies to communicate successes in the school district and to communicate which areas of operations need improvement. The information presented was honest and data driven. Areas of deficiencies in academic achievement were identified and discussed. All information was supported by qualitative and quantitative data—only the facts.

Once the plan was established, consistent and regularly scheduled communication about the district was assured. A variety of mediums were selected to communicate issues. For example, the school district web page was redesigned so that it was more interactive and told the district's "story." It was updated daily, and each district-level director was charged with the task of providing relevant information on each departmental site.

The Communication Specialist position was reclassified to Public Information Officer, and daily press releases about school system happenings were issued. Board meetings were redesigned to allow board members and the superintendent to give informational progress reports at the beginning of the meeting. Reporters were briefed at each meeting. Additionally, an annual report was developed titled "Realizing the Vision," which detailed progress on the school district's vision plan. This report was used as a point of discussion at all community and civic meetings.

As part of the proactive nature of the plan, the state school board association was asked to facilitate a community gathering of 250 stakeholders called "What Counts." The forum was a way to gather input and a way to check in with community members, parents, teachers, and staff to ensure that the vision plan was aligned with community expectations. In collaboration with the Chamber of Commerce, the superintendent delivered an annual State of the School System Address in November to 225 business and community leaders. Also, a parent link phone system and a student information management system was purchased and used to connect parents and community members with upcoming events and activities.

All of these items worked in concert to communicate the strengths and needs of a school district. The communication plan was a stepping-off point to greater school district success and community support. The concerted planning effort resulted in two major benefits: budget items were realigned to address the needs of students and every school in the district made Adequate

Yearly Progress (AYP) that year. The conclusion is that if a superintendent fully understands the need to communicate effectively, then the process of improved academic achievement for all students is accelerated.

Advice:

It is better to overcommunicate than undercommunicate with school district stakeholders. Telling the public about an issue of concern is a good strategy; once an area of concern is identified, it is essential that a brief but thoughtful plan of action is also presented for public review. The public gains confidence in leadership when they feel informed and are aware of plans to help address weaknesses.

Tip: Don't Succumb to Pressure to Violate the Data Practices Act

At the top of the list of things a superintendent absolutely does not want to have to address is inappropriate behavior of a staff member toward boys or girls. Once such behavior comes to the superintendent's attention, two things must happen immediately: the police are involved (if they aren't already) and the staff member is suspended pending investigation. When the media becomes aware of an issue, it is a delicate balance between the public's right to know and the rights of the alleged offender.

Example:

A local police chief (there were five municipalities in the school district) contacted the superintendent to let him know that a complaint had just been filed against a person employed by the school district. The complaint was for using the Internet to show pornography to an underage girl and attempting to entice her to meet with him. The police notified the superintendent in the late afternoon. The employee was part-time, working the evening shift. The police came to the school at which the person worked and took him into custody. The police also confiscated the person's work computer. Fortunately, this was after school hours and not observed by many people.

The police blotter showed the action taken at one of the district schools. It was just a matter of time before the media would be at the superintendent's door. The complication to this circumstance was that the complaint against the person came from a different state (a mother filed it on behalf of her minor daughter). By the next afternoon, a national news media reporter contacted the superintendent. The superintendent could only respond that little or no information could be shared by the district because of the ongoing police investigation.

For district residents, the superintendent crafted a letter for the paper explaining that, until the individual taken into custody was charged, any comments by the school district could jeopardize the investigation. Parents had begun calling the superintendent's office to complain that they should have been informed, and they wanted to know more details and have greater assurance that their children were safe.

The individual was charged by the police; the work computer was found to be "clean." Apparently the person did not engage in any inappropriate behavior from work, nor was there evidence he had inappropriate contact with any girls within the state.

The letter to the public explained the rationale and restrictions that guide issues such as this one. The superintendent's communication was clear, understandable, and pointed out the downsides of revealing too much information too soon in legal issues. The superintendent could not, in good faith, provide a statement to the community that there was no chance the person had any contact with a student in the district—even though there was no evidence that a district student had been involved. Not all parents were happy with the superintendent's response.

The fact is, if too much information was provided by the superintendent in the media, the case against this person could very well have been compromised. The need to inform was offset by the need to make sure a guilty person would not go free because of something said on TV or radio.

Advice:

School superintendents are not detectives, police officers, or attorneys. Trying to interpret the law or make a judgment about appropriate or inappropriate comments in a police investigation is beyond the span of superintendent responsibility. If ever in doubt about how to proceed in a legal situation, contact the school district attorney. However, common sense in determining when, what, and how to connect with parents, the public, and the news media should prevail.

Tip: Plan and Organize Committees Well

Many administrators recognize the benefit of community involvement with their schools. Committee participation is one way parents, students, and other community residents can be part of school and district planning and decision making. Committees can certainly be helpful to a superintendent and school board; however, when committees go awry, the result can be disastrous. Well-structured committees help enhance school-community relations.

Example:

Due to some past events related to previous leadership, a new superintendent was well aware that he needed to work hard on gaining the trust and respect of both "internal" and "external" clients. Because the district was located in a suburban growth corridor, planning for this future growth was a priority. Several goals were immediately apparent to the superintendent:

• Improve technology (hardware, software, building-to-building equity)
• Assess facility needs (space and condition)
• Develop a matrix of existing programs and services for preschool and special education student populations (there was great confusion about the model used to serve these populations)
• Project enrollments, revenue, expenditures for the next five years

In each area, the superintendent formed either a small task force or larger representative committee to gather and review information to ultimately make advisory recommendations to the superintendent and/or school board.

For technology, the committee included teacher representatives from each building, support staff in library/media, administration, parents, and school board. The superintendent identified the type of representation for the committee, the charge, the meeting structure, and intended outcomes. Cochairs were identified at the first meeting. The committee was advisory to the superintendent.

Assessment of facility needs eventually resulted in the creation of a representative committee (teachers, support staff, students, elected city officials, local business owners, and parents). Again, the superintendent determined the committee structure, charge, meeting frequency/dates/times, and wrote the agendas. The superintendent chaired this committee and provided the bulk of the information to the committee for their review. The committee was charged with making facility recommendations that would be brought to the school board for their consideration.

For the analysis of programs and services, the superintendent formed a task force of special education teachers and parents and charged them with developing a matrix by grade and school of special education programs, services, and remedial/intervention programs and services. Staffing for each program or service was also recorded. A separate task force was formed for preschool education programs and services. Members of the task force were early childhood special education teachers, paraprofessional staff, and parents. Both of these ad hoc committees reported directly to the superintendent.

The last goal was met by using state demographer models and current district numbers to project the enrollments. Revenue and expenditures were projected using the business office software programs. This goal area was part of administrative team agendas and discussion. The administrative team members gathered and analyzed needed information and made recommendations in conjunction with the superintendent about future facility and staffing needs.

The superintendent worked with committees and task forces to gather, review, and interpret information important to the schools and a growing school community. The results from each study group assisted in putting plans together to improve technology; to construct new schools and renovate existing spaces; to plan for increases in preschool and special education populations programs; and to be able to plan for funding future programs, services, and facility needs.

Advice:

Committees can be an ideal way for community and school representatives to be involved in how schools operate. The superintendent determines how committees are structured, their charge, and to whom they report. Every committee in a school is advisory. A well-run committee can boost the image of a school or district, leaving participants satisfied with their work. A poorly run committee with unclear expectations can create the opposite result—a poor image of the school/district and dissatisfaction with participation.

Chapter Six

Monitoring Efficient Operations

A superintendent of schools is held accountable for having the knowledge and skill to manage a multitude of complex operational functions. Few CEOs in the private sector have such demanding and varied responsibilities. Operational functions such as food service, transportation, budgeting and accounting, facilities management, health and safety, technology, and asset management are vital to a successful school organization. In many districts, the superintendent is the person in charge of one or more of the areas mentioned above. In large districts, the superintendent supervises others who hold the responsibility. Either way, the operational side of the school organization demands as much attention from the superintendent as does the academic side.

REVIEW AND ASSESS OPERATIONAL FUNCTIONS

New superintendents spend time studying and evaluating all aspects of operations. The effectiveness and efficiency of the organization depend on how well defined key processes are within each department. These processes can be examined and evaluated as distinct functions within the organization but, the bottom line is, they must work in tandem to keep the system operating at its best. For example, there are a few key indicators that assist a new superintendent in determining the effectiveness and efficiency of personnel functions. These include:

- Current and clearly defined job descriptions for noncertified staff
- Hiring practices that promote selection of the most qualified candidates

- Supervisors who understand their role in providing feedback to employees to help improve job performance and operational efficiency
- Probationary time periods for all new employees to determine feasibility of retention
- Staff training and development to keep employees up-to-date on equipment, procedures, regulations, and innovative practices
- Supportive, respectful work environment between and among noncertified and certified staff
- Supervisor knowledge of union contracts
- Nonretention of poorly performing employees
- Employee understanding of the connection of work performed to the educational mission of the district
- Strategic plans that include short- and long-term goals and measured accomplishments toward district goals

This is not a comprehensive list of indicators of the "health" of operational functions in personnel, but the items listed help to evaluate the effectiveness, efficiency, and structure of this particular district operation. For each aspect of the district operations, the superintendent is obligated to assess established processes, practices, and procedures to determine how well those support the organization and its effectiveness.

ASSURE REGULATORY AND LEGAL COMPLIANCE

Each major area of operation has regulations, resources, standards, guidelines, and community expectations. State and federal laws regulate food service, transportation, special education, and the work environment, while maintenance, cleaning, clerical functions, and technology are influenced by district policies, contracts, and by state, county, or local agencies. To complicate matters further, many of the legal and regulatory functions change with each new legislative session. Designated state, local, or federal agencies have the power and obligation to oversee the broad area of operation for schools or businesses.

It is not uncommon that some operational functions are outsourced or contracted thereby shifting responsibility for compliance to the contractor. In those instances, superintendents must be vigilant to assure legal and regulatory compliance is addressed in contracts or agreements. Whether a district relies on the superintendent, supervisory personnel, or a contractor to oversee an operational function, keeping up-to-date on regulatory and legal compliance is essential.

COMMUNICATE WITH THE BUSINESS OFFICE

Communication between the superintendent and the business office should be frequent and purposeful. New superintendents can learn much from the business office staff about the way the district operates, its priorities, resources, and traditions. The business manager can provide perspectives on barriers to efficient operations and initiatives for improvement.

In tough budget times, communication with the business official becomes especially important to pinpoint revenues and expenditures through well-defined processes so that the impact of any budgetary adjustment (i.e., cut) is as accurate as possible. The business office should have up-to-date management software and well-trained employees on the use of the software. Data on virtually every aspect of district operations should be available, allowing for scrutiny. For example, software programs can provide up-to-date tracking of enrollments and staffing—which is very important to budget accuracy.

The most recent audit report is a good source of budget information. The superintendent should be aware of the auditor findings as soon as the report is drafted. The audit report is extremely important because it shows how effectively the district plans, manages, and adjusts for annual revenues and expenditures. It also shows how efficient the district is, and has been, in monitoring key budgeting functions. The audit results are reported to the school board; the board approves the audit report. Any recommendations from the auditors must be addressed, and these recommendations become the responsibility of the superintendent.

With limited resources facing most districts, expectations for accuracy, information gathering and analysis, and adherence to regulatory standards in business office practices are more important than ever. Responsibility for business office operations ultimately rests with the superintendent.

CONSIDER PARTNERSHIPS

Increasing numbers of superintendents are seeking partnerships with other districts or agencies to share costs or responsibility for district operations. Group purchasing, joint powers agreements for limited but defined services, cooperative arrangements for staff training and itinerant staff contracts, colocated services that benefit both parties (for example, city and school maintenance offices and equipment storage) can provide the support needed to reduce costs rather than services. New superintendents are collaborative leaders willing to explore unique opportunities to maximize resources. Partnerships are replacing parochialism. Cooperation is replacing competition.

To be most effective, these efforts are beneficial to all partners, are planned well, and are monitored frequently.

VALUE ALL EMPLOYEES

Employees in operational functions are typically nonlicensed personnel and comprise about half of the organization's workforce. In many districts, these employees reside in the school district in greater numbers than do teaching or administrative staff. Noncertified employees can and do have tremendous influence on how community residents regard the school district. Bus drivers, custodians, food service staff, clerical employees, aides, and other nonlicensed staff can be great supporters of the organization for which they work or the most vocal critics. Their work experiences are shared with friends, family, and neighbors. Public perceptions of how well the district functions and how taxpayer dollars are spent can be dramatically affected by what district employees say about their employer (the district).

New superintendents may find the following ideas helpful in developing positive working relationships with noncertified employees:

- Visit areas that are the home base for many noncertified employees. Kitchens, custodial offices, maintenance and bus garages, and school offices are examples.
- Make a point to know as many names of department and area supervisors as possible.
- Be familiar with the nature of the work performed by employees.
- Listen when visiting with noncertified employees. Ask questions about their work.
- Keep each employee group informed about district goals, status, and initiatives. Many noncertified employees feel left out of the "loop." Set informational meetings at their work sites or a place and time of their choosing.
- Compliment work well done.
- Make a connection about the importance of their work to the purpose of the organization and its students.
- Model respectful behavior—especially when students are present. Do not tolerate disrespect toward any employee.
- Assure that supervisors of operations are trained in the performance review process.
- Hire the most qualified people for nonlicensed positions.
- Encourage innovation and new ideas to increase effectiveness and efficiency.

- Feature food service, transportation, custodial services, paraprofessional work, and clerical personnel in newsletters and on websites.

It is impossible to have all employees happy with their job. But, when employees know the value of the work they do, and have a sense that those "at the top" also value their work, job satisfaction becomes more likely.

BE A LEADER AND A MANAGER

A superintendent "leader" inspires others to accept and embrace the district's vision and to take action to achieve the goals beneficial to the mission of the organization. A superintendent "manager" assures that others meet performance expectations and keeps the organization functioning with effectiveness and efficiency. Managers oversee the work of the organization; leaders oversee the vision for the organization. Both are essential; the responsibilities of the position require that the superintendent be both a manager and a leader.

An important leadership role for the superintendent is to assure that district staff see and understand the connection between how the district operates and the successful pursuit of the district vision. "Schools departments, individual teachers—actually every program and person in the system need to be pursuing their own creative and challenging vision. But it all begins with a *system* vision" (Schwahn and Spady, 2001, p. 128). Through discussion, meetings, evaluations, and data analysis, the superintendent can influence how supervisors and support staff view the importance of their work and whether they see the relationship of their work to the students and their success.

Superintendents in virtually every school system in the nation are looking for ways to cut operational costs. Some typical cost-cutting measures include: reducing or eliminating bus routes; outsourcing financial, personnel, and maintenance services; contracting food service or transportation; seeking energy savings; and forming cooperative purchasing units with other districts. It is a fact that "savings from bulk purchasing of fuel oil, milk, paper, athletic equipment, technology and other supplies have been gained through cooperative agreements among school districts" (Jazzar and Algozzine, 2006, p. 147). This cooperative spirit is somewhat new for many district leaders; but survival is a strong motivator to cooperate rather than compete.

Superintendents in all parts of the nation are faced with aging district facilities and the possibility of closing one or more buildings due to declining enrollment and/or inability to carry operational costs of underused facilities. The condition of the nation's school facilities is abysmal. According to the U.S. Department of Education in a report in 1999, the price tag for bringing the nation's schools to "good overall condition" was estimated to be about $127 billion. This is a challenge that has no quick or easy solution.

To maintain educational programs and services, some communities may have to face the closing of neighborhood schools or losing schools altogether under district consolidation. These are tough issues for any superintendent, school board, and school community to address. Courage to do the right thing, even knowing how difficult it is for the community, is a quality a superintendent simply must have given today's budget climate.

MANAGE DISTRICT FINANCES

One of the most difficult and disappointing aspects of a superintendent's responsibility is managing finances. There simply are not enough resources for the programs and services needed to assure academic success for all students. Whether considered a wealthy district or poor, meeting individual student needs results in competition for available dollars and allocation of resources to the highest priority issues.

Several financial challenges face school districts today. One is that decreasing revenue is occurring simultaneously with increasing expectations. Another is the increasing cost of providing very specialized services to a growing number of students. A third is that voters are not receptive to tax increases for any reason, even if it means the survival of their community school district. A fourth is enrollment in many rural areas is steadily declining as families and graduates move to larger cities for employment or higher education opportunities. And, lastly, public education has been thrust into partisan politics subject to both fair and unfair scrutiny. Media reports have had a role in shaping public opinion about the efficacy of public schools, and subsequently, whether they "deserve" to have more funding.

To meet these challenges, expenses need to be cut or reduced. Budget reduction is a process that requires planning. Prior to starting the process, the superintendent provides information to the school board and community about trend data (at least five years) on revenue and expenditures; trend data (at least five years) on enrollments by grade; projected enrollment and revenue for a three- to five-year time period; student achievement data (at least five years); and matrixes illustrating programs added over the last five years to meet individual and small group student needs.

It is eye opening to illustrate the costs that have escalated over recent years (health insurance, fuel, utilities, special education, for example) and what has already been done to reduce costs. In other words, the budget reduction process is not isolated activity occurring without clear explanation of where the district has been, what it is doing, and what is needed to continue to serve all students. Once budget reduction becomes necessary, some suggestions may help facilitate the process.

- Conduct a work-study session with the school board to establish criteria for budget reduction.
- Develop a plan to gather input on budget reduction ideas.
- Develop a method to categorize suggestions and cost estimates.
- Weigh suggestions against criteria and cost savings.
- Analyze reduction suggestions in terms of impact to student achievement.
- Think of ways to increase revenue, not just cut expenditures.
- Differentiate and prioritize among mandated, essential, and "nice to have" programs and services.
- Communicate issues clearly with district stakeholders. Graphs help.

Not all reduction ideas fit every district. One district may implement a cost reduction measure that does not produce the same result in another district. Also, look for real savings. For example, cutting some programs may result in families leaving the district to seek the program elsewhere. In that instance, anticipate the revenue lost as well as cost savings.

ESSENCE OF MONITORING EFFICIENT OPERATIONS

Successful superintendents know and understand the relationship between the operation side of education and improving the learning environment for all students. Noncertified employees are an important part of district success. Continuous improvement and clear job expectations should be emphasized in facilitating efficient district operations. Exploring innovative, creative, and cost-effective measures is essential to managing district operations. Budget difficulties plague nearly every school district. Be armed with data and a planning process to avoid random and arbitrary decisions.

TIPS AND ADVICE

Tip: Prepare Employees Well

Supervision of employees is a skill that requires development and training. When a supervisor is hired and part of that person's responsibility is to evaluate the performance of others, care should be taken to make sure the supervisor is prepared to conduct employee evaluations.

Example:

A superintendent of a growing district created a new district office position, Supervisor of Buildings and Grounds. This position was created for several reasons: the existing facilities were aging, needing repairs and renovations; at least one and probably two new schools would be added over the next six years; much of the maintenance in the school buildings had been outsourced and the cost of outsourcing was escalating; a five-year maintenance plan was needed; new health and safety requirements were emerging each year from the legislature; and one of the planning goals the superintendent set when she arrived in the district was to assure effectiveness and efficiency in the buildings, grounds, and custodial areas. Once a qualified person was hired for the new position, that individual would be responsible for monitoring efficiencies and supervising the head custodians in each building.

The superintendent selected a very qualified person for the position, but the individual had little experience in employee supervision and conducting performance reviews. The superintendent encouraged the person to attend a series of management sessions that she knew would be beneficial.

Before the new supervisor had his first conference with a head custodian (one the supervisor did not believe was performing at expected levels), the superintendent met with the new supervisor and had him conduct a mock conference with her to help him prepare. She then provided feedback about what was said, how it was said, and suggestions to help the "real" conference meet intended goals. For example, during the mock conference, the new supervisor had identified three strengths of the head custodian and forty-three areas for improvement. The superintendent encouraged the new supervisor to categorize the forty-three individual items into two or three main areas so that the person being evaluated would not be totally overwhelmed with so many items to improve.

The superintendent also helped the new supervisor develop the connection between buildings and grounds and the educational mission. She made sure the Supervisor of Buildings and Grounds attended the administrative team meetings once a month. At these meetings the supervisor could participate in discussions with principals about a variety of issues affecting educational programs and students. Important issues learned at these meetings were passed on to the head custodians by the supervisor at their monthly meetings. These types of connections help improve the effectiveness of operations.

Advice:

Every employee has a job to do in and for the organization. Preparing employees for their job is as important as evaluating employees' performance in doing their job.

Tip: Safety is Truly Job One

The importance of a five-year facility plan cannot be overstated. This plan, when thorough and updated each year, can save the district thousands of dollars in emergency repairs or replacements. Not only that, safety is enhanced when plans are in place because many potentially hazardous situations are alleviated.

Example:

About three months after a superintendent came on board, a large portion of the middle school roof collapsed during a heavy rainstorm in the summer. Fortunately, no adults or students were in the building. Upon investigation, several key factors contributed to this crisis situation.

1. The building was over thirty years old and still had the original roof.
2. There had been two additions to the one-story building.
3. The roof was patched—patches over patches.
4. There had been leaks before, but those were quickly patched over.
5. There had been very little maintenance completed on any of the building. If repairs were done, it was primarily in a reactionary sense.
6. There was no five-year maintenance plan.

The roof issue prompted the superintendent to investigate all maintenance, health, safety, and general facility conditions. It was apparent that the roof, boilers, vehicles, HVAC systems, and cleaning equipment all suffered from neglect—not the type that was really visible, but hidden neglect. For example, HVAC system filters weren't changed because custodians didn't know how to do that; used or rebuilt parts were installed in equipment—repeatedly—to avoid replacing with new; employees did most of the roof and boiler repairs and not all were qualified to do so; employees were using equipment that they did not receive any training on how to use properly and safely.

A list of all maintenance and facility needs, estimated costs, and level of urgency was developed. Once the highest priority items were identified, projects were put into a five-year plan. It was determined that some of the issues would be covered with capital dollars, some under performance contracts, some through energy savings, and some through an upcoming bond referendum.

Because a portion of the middle school roof had collapsed and water had seeped in or actually flooded a large part of one end of the building, the structure was closed off to any unauthorized persons. Environmental specialists were called to assess the building for mold and other air quality issues.

Bids were taken for roof replacement and for abatement of mold. Other bids were taken for repair of the facility. Classrooms were reassigned and student schedules altered so that most of the students could start school in the other portions of the building in September. Five classrooms of students were shifted to another facility. Students and parents were notified, and bus schedules were set up to transfer students each day from one building to another (and during the day for their specialist classes). By December, all of the work was completed, so students moved back to the middle school.

Advice:

Delaying investment in infrastructure may cost more in the long run and not just in dollars, but in disruption to the educational program for students. Be proactive and address the highest priority concerns. Keep the public informed about safety, facilities, and the impact on learning environments.

Tip: Value All Employees

A superintendent who takes time to meet, greet, and involve nonlicensed and itinerant employees is more likely viewed as a "real person" rather than a bureaucrat. When employees feel valued and connected to the purpose of the organization, it is likely that higher productivity and better morale is the result.

Example:

The superintendent of a large, suburban school district always made sure that he visited each school site at least twice a year. Prior to going to a building, he looked through the student yearbook from the previous year because the yearbooks allowed the superintendent to look up staff that he wanted to make sure he could greet by name once in the schools. These included the office clerical staff—especially the principal secretary (administrative assistant), the head or lead custodian, and the head cook or lead person in the kitchen. The superintendent would make it a point to visit the office, kitchen, and custodial room and to speak with the staff in those areas.

The superintendent also participated in a portion of the orientation each year for new faculty and attended the required training for bus drivers, custodians, and paraprofessionals in health and safety issues. The superintendent always stopped by the orientation for substitute teachers, and in his second year in the district, he changed the name of the substitute orientation to Reserve Teacher Orientation (which was very positively received by the participants).

Each year, the superintendent looked for at least one way to improve connections with nonlicensed and itinerant staff. Over a five-year time period, handbooks for new employees were developed, reserve teachers each had a folder of school and district information (including maps to the school sites), bus drivers received training on discipline and proper restraint of students, food service staff received coordinated training on kitchen safety and food preparation, paraprofessional staff received updated handbooks containing procedural and policy information (data privacy, due process, confidentiality), and custodians either attended or viewed (new video) blood-borne pathogen training. CPR and AED training was made available to all staff.

The superintendent spoke to principals, union representatives, and food service and custodial supervisors to find the best time each fall to come to the building or location identified to meet with their groups to give a brief update about district goals, new initiatives, or a general school business overview. This same type of meeting occurred again in the spring.

In this district, nonlicensed employees went the extra mile for the district and their school because they were very proud of their work. They knew their "boss" appreciated their efforts because he told them so every chance he could.

Advice:

Running an effective and efficient organization is not just about the bottom line. People impact quality of service, efficiency of budgets, and image of the organization. Employees who feel valued are much more willing to go the "extra mile" in their work. The superintendent can and does influence how employees feel about their jobs. Knowing an employee's name is one simple way to let employees know he/she is valued.

Tip: Avoid Being First in Some Things

Think through the "worst case scenario" of adopting something that puts the district in the position of being "first" to participate in a new program. Even a strong rationale for trying the new idea may go over very well with the public (or media).

Example:

There are two different examples that fit with this tip. One is that several superintendents were contacted by their state department to participate in the purchase of a federal commodity—irradiated ground beef—for their food service program. The product was considered healthier than regular ground beef. Some districts did agree to participate because of the health benefit to students (no chance of E. coli).

The media caught the story of "irradiated beef" in schools. The publicity and how the product was portrayed caused many parents to become upset because they associated irradiated beef with radiation, which, of course, was not true. Many superintendents, who were thinking of the health benefits for students, were forced to drop the program under parental pressure. Trust in leadership suffered a blow even though it was really an unfair fight.

The other issue involved an opportunity to obtain state-of-the-art fitness equipment. The company said that if the district purchased the equipment and agreed to track participants and fitness data, the company would pay back the district, month by month, over ten years, for the total cost of the equipment. School districts did receive the high-quality equipment, and many did receive at least one or two years of monthly payments from the company.

Within two years, the participating school districts were informed by the attorney general's office that the company was being investigated for fraud. The owners were charged with conspiracy to commit fraud and were convicted and jailed. The districts that purchased the equipment still kept the equipment. The downside for them was that there would be no payments coming in the future from the company. The good news was that there were so many districts involved (duped) that it did not appear that any one in particular was singled out. The bad news is that many districts paid out thousands of dollars for equipment they otherwise may not have purchased.

Advice:

A superintendent cannot always know when a good idea, one that makes sense and seems fiscally responsible, may create a firestorm of controversy. But thinking through "what is the worst thing that could happen if we did this?" may help in the decision-making process. There certainly are circumstances beyond the control or expectation of a superintendent and school board. In those cases, tell the truth to the public and move on.

Tip: Tough Decisions Need Careful Planning

In the climate of little or no new money to help defray inflationary costs, district leaders have to consider the possibility of collaboration or consolidation. The press to address the needs of the students forces the discussion and the possibility.

Example:

A superintendent of a small district had been in the district three years. He realized that the enrollment was continuing to decline and if projections were correct, in two years there would only be 285 students in K–12. He contacted three neighboring districts to see if they had an interest in looking at the feasibility of consolidation. Two of the districts were supportive, and the third was a reluctant participant. The school boards of each district were involved in the decision to look at whether or not they may need to consolidate. A study of the districts (conducted by a consulting firm with experience in feasibility studies of consolidation) proved that it would be beneficial for students and taxpayers if at least two of the districts consolidated.

The feasibility study prompted further action to look in more detail at the two more willing districts' contracts, course offerings, schedules, transportation system, debt, revenue projections, and enrollments. These are just a few of the major areas that need to be addressed in a consolidation.

The communities were involved in the study process, and the consulting firm interviewed many of the community business and governmental leaders. All board members were interviewed, and a sampling of parents and staff were invited to participate in the interview/survey process. The consulting firm suggested a broad-based committee with representatives from each community to participate in several meetings to hear about the feasibility study results and to make advisory recommendations to each of the school boards.

The result was that the community committee did recommend pursuing consolidation. The school boards acted on the recommendation. The consolidation would be complete in two years.

The superintendent will be out of a job since the two districts will combine and the other superintendent is more senior (that is how the school boards decided to select the superintendent). But the superintendent who will be "out" has two years to pursue another position. Students will benefit from the addition of classes at the high school level—in both districts due to more students per grade level. Some staff may lose their positions, but the planning process will allow for time to at least look around for other positions. The districts are considering early retirement incentives in both districts. That may help retain younger staff. The point is, once the issue was identified, the superintendent stepped up and took action to do what is best for students.

Advice:

Once the signs of distress are visible, superintendents take action to minimize the impact of a future change, like consolidation, through planning ahead. Student needs, both current and future, are the highest priority. Do what needs to be done but make sure the planning process is sufficient to allow for input and attainable outcomes.

Tip: There Are Times to Make Concessions

Not all decisions are made because of efficiency and effectiveness. Some are made just because they are the right and humane thing to do.

Example:

A veteran support staff member was transferred from lunch duty in one elementary school to playground supervision at another site because of staff balance at the two schools. Within weeks of her new assignment, she was not performing her duties well.

The principal at the new site followed contract provisions and a progressive discipline. The employee seemed to disregard the provisions of the corrective action plan, appearing confused by the nature of the stated concerns. Ultimately, a termination plan was developed and processed through the district office. The superintendent's involvement up to that time had been advisory in nature.

The employee contacted the superintendent's office and asked to meet with the superintendent. She asked if it was OK to bring her husband. Though initially hesitant, the superintendent agreed.

The couple entered the office nervous but respectful. Surprisingly, it was the husband who began to speak, indicating that they were struggling to accept "what is happening." The superintendent fought off an initial surge of cynicism, for it was wrongly assumed he was about to defend his wife's performance. But that was not the case.

The husband explained that his wife had recently been diagnosed as having initial stages of Alzheimer's disease, and he pulled a wrinkled and worn doctor's note from his pocket to confirm the condition. He said that his spouse could still function effectively within long-held routines, but she was increasingly challenged with new environments and unique situations. The change in both building and work assignment proved to be too much, and she could not, he admitted, be successful in her current role.

What the pair sought was to maintain her dignity. On behalf of his wife, who sat quietly and sadly beside him, a resignation was offered up as an alternative to the termination plan. The superintendent was touched by the honesty, honored to share in a deeply personal story, and moved by the sacrificial resolve. The superintendent wondered aloud if the old assignment might still be a possibility.

The superintendent offered that a return to the lunchroom position would be considered if they thought she could fulfill the responsibilties. There were contracts and confidences to keep as well as budget considerations and staff balances. But the decision to move a veteran employee, struggling with a life-altering condition, back to a place where there was some likelihood for success won out over economics in the end. Termination proceedings ceased.

The couple promised that they would look to the district for the clear signal of when keeping her in the lunchroom position was no longer an option, especially due to the progressive nature of the disease.

Advice:

Making reasonable accommodations for employees so they can be successful in their work is always a goal of supervision. When challenges occur, honest discussions help define the parameters for employee performance and their success. Students are the first priority; looking for humane and reasonable options on behalf of a staff member is a priority also.

Chapter Seven

Thinking Strategically

Although not every issue can be anticipated, much of a superintendent's time is spent gathering and processing information to assess situations or circumstances that could impact students, schools, or the district in general. Not only do superintendents think about potential problems and their possible solutions; they also develop proactive measures to avert or minimize negative outcomes. Thinking strategically requires consistent analysis of both short- and long-term issues, problems, solutions, and options.

Leaders who ascribe to systems thinking understand that the effectiveness and efficiency of the school organization is affected by decisions made at every level in the system. To think about issues from a strategic or systems approach provides "... a framework for seeing interrelationships rather than things, for seeing patterns of change rather than static snapshots" (Jazzar and Algozzine, 2006, p. 25). Thinking strategically facilitates proactive leadership, which, in turn, is essential for anticipating issues that affect the organization.

RELY ON THE ADMINISTRATIVE TEAM

A close working relationship with principals, directors, and assistants provides access to critical information to help anticipate current and potential issues. Administrative team meetings facilitate the development of trust, teamwork, and communication among team members and the superintendent. Informed and involved administrative team members can explain and promote district priorities to their staff that, in turn, helps contain rumors and misinformation.

Superintendents use administrative meetings to tap into the "front line" of district operations and activities. Each meeting allows administrators to talk about their area, including progress toward goals, special events, potential problems, and resolved issues. It is in one of the first administrative team meetings that a new superintendent sets the expectation that he/she be given a "heads up" regarding issues or situations that could escalate in intensity, impacting students, a school, or the district.

The administrative group also serves as a sounding board regarding direction and change. District and building level administrators are key communicators with staff and parents. They are aware of staff morale and specific issues that affect staff or parent attitudes toward policy, procedure, or educational methodologies. This is helpful in determining what concerns should be addressed as the district moves forward in planning, and what change initiatives may be most needed.

The superintendent constantly gathers information and data from the administrative team, analyzes and synthesizes it, and uses it to plan strategically. However, not all information is helpful, and not all data is worth analyzing. Guthrie and Schuermann (2010) found that the executive who is strategic in his or her leadership knows the purposes for which data are collected and ensures that those purposes are met. The superintendent relies on the administrative team to gather and use data that tie directly to the district's mission and to the strategic planning goals.

DEVELOP "WHAT IF" SCENARIOS

A key strategy in reducing or even avoiding some problems is developing "what if" scenarios. In this strategy, the superintendent thinks through potential reactions or outcomes to one or more solutions to any given problem or concern.

When a problem or situation arises, the superintendent determines options or possible solutions. He/she then thinks about the impact or possible "fall out" of any particular solution. It is possible that the right decision regarding an issue or concern can help avoid further problems. On the other hand, a particular decision or solution may create more problems than existed before. For example, if a parent wants his/her child moved to a different teacher and the principal has said no, the parent takes the situation to the next level, the superintendent. The superintendent thinks about these questions: What if I reverse the principal's decision? What are the ramifications for the principal beyond this particular issue if I take any action? What if I actually agree that the child should be moved? What if I send the issue back to the building principal without any decision on my part? What if I agree with the principal and the parent moves to the board level? What if the decision sets a precedent for other such parent requests?

The use of "what if" scenarios may not lead to the right decision, but they help the superintendent prepare for possible reaction as a result of the decision.

KEEP THE SCHOOL BOARD INFORMED

The savvy superintendent keeps the school board apprised of issues that have the potential for negative or controversial public reaction. Frequent and regular communication with the school board keeps them informed about those types of situations and also about less volatile issues. This communication could be an email, memo, or voice mail, but it should not be specific to board agenda items (which could be interpreted as influencing board decisions). Frequent, brief, factual information communicated to the school board on a regular basis (a board update) keeps the board apprised of events, activities, and potential problems.

School board members like to know in advance if they might be receiving calls from the public about a particular issue. They also appreciate facts related to an issue. The role of school board members is not to solve district problems outside of the board table. They are, however, entitled to be prepared should constituents contact them. School board members should not be blindsided on significant district concerns.

In communicating potential issues with the board, the superintendent provides information about what he/she is doing to address the issue. The school board expects the superintendent to be proactive and to use his/her administrative skills to ameliorate troublesome issues. Informing the board of potential issues is a good strategy; outlining a plan of action to address the issue if it lands on the board table is just as important.

HAVE COURAGE

One of the reasons that so few people know or understand what a superintendent really does is that so much of his/her work is behind the scenes. Not even principals are usually aware of the time a superintendent spends in analyzing volumes of information in order to keep the district on course and averting disaster.

A superintendent is privy to a host of information about every aspect of the school district. Areas for which the superintendent maintains oversight include: personnel, food service, transportation, facilities, safety, custodial, special education, finances, legal issues, policies and practices, federal and state mandates, student achievement, extracurricular options, course offerings and curricular articulation, technology use, enrollment, demographics, gifted education, remedial education, alternative education, and community education.

The superintendent uses information from the administrative team, staff, and specific data sources to think about what issues could potentially derail progress toward meeting educational goals. This is a "twenty-four seven" responsibility. Successful superintendents not only are aware of (and anticipate) these issues but they also have the courage to address them as soon as they become aware of the possibility of a negative impact on students or the organization in general.

For example, a new superintendent in a district that had aging, neglected facilities anticipates greater and greater expenditures for repair and upkeep. This situation is a budget issue, but it also could be a health and safety issue. The new superintendent gathers reliable information, develops a plan of action, and requires immediate repair of potentially harmful facility conditions. There is risk in "going public" regarding safety or health concerns, but there is greater risk in not addressing an issue until after a traumatic event has occurred. Having the courage to tackle such issues, before a crisis event occurs, is necessary.

Not all district issues are as visible as facility conditions. However, these can be just as damaging to the educational environment for students and staff if left unchecked. These types of issues pertain to policies, practices, and traditions. Having the courage to change a policy or practice that is outdated, inappropriate, or worse yet, violates a recent law is as important for the strategic leader as anticipating and changing something more obvious. Once aware of a potential problem, a superintendent is obligated to investigate and take action if necessary.

THINK ABOUT IMPACT OF DECISIONS

Not every decision has the potential for a negative outcome. Sadly, however, many do. When confronted with a decision, superintendents think through what the worst thing is that could happen as a result of the decision. However, that doesn't mean a good decision needs to be rejected because of a potentially negative outcome. It simply means to be aware of, and prepare for, the impact of some decisions on the organization and school community. Caruth and Handlogen (2000) write about the importance of evaluating every decision in terms of costs and benefits, or, just as important, in terms of the risks involved and the results obtained.

Superintendents soon realize that not every issue or decision can be a high priority. In the process of thinking through the impact of a decision, it may be wise to compromise, give in, or adopt what the majority seems to want or need. To do so is not a show of weakness, but rather a realization that the issue itself is not one that deserves a fight to the end to prove a point. Ego and emotions can sometimes interfere with sound decision making. Knowing this and stepping back from the issue for a while is helpful. A perspective of what is best for students and the organization keeps superintendents focused on the mission of the district; not on every issue brought to the superintendent's desk deserves a high-priority rating.

It is a responsibility of superintendents to protect their administrators and the school board from doing things that could have dire consequences later. What seems like a good decision at the time may prove to be a poor decision for the future. For example, it may seem innocent enough to both a principal and a staff member if they and their spouses are seen socializing in the community on occasion. Some staff may have a concern about the principal having "favorites" as a result of the periodic social relationship between the couples. The superintendent may dismiss the concern as unimportant, or the superintendent may choose to have a conversation with the principal to raise his awareness of the situation. The decision to address the issue or not is one that the superintendent makes by thinking through how much the issue impairs the principal's ability to be an effective leader in his building.

In another scenario, the superintendent can help the school board understand the impact on them, their reputation, the administrators, and future decisions if they capitulate (or worse yet, reverse a decision) because angry parents confront them at a school board meeting. Superintendents take the time to prepare their board with good information and strategies to address the issue of controversy at a school board meeting.

Often, the superintendent knows when an issue may draw a crowd and forewarns the school board. A reminder to the school board chair about previously discussed operating principles (how to organize the public forum for large groups who want to address an issue with the school board) is another proactive measure that helps reduce or eliminate chaos at a school board meeting.

ESSENCE OF THINKING STRATEGICALLY

Anticipating issues helps a superintendent think through possible outcomes of actions or decisions on the school community. He/she weighs the issue and possible options to address the issue against what is best for the organization and the long-term impact on students. Decisions sometimes become disastrous when adult needs are given higher priority status than students' needs or when unanticipated results occur. Anticipating issues often leads to interventions that prevent worst possible scenarios. Informed decision makers, strategic thinkers, focus on facts and information, not emotions. A superintendent cannot avoid all negative impacts of decisions, but he/she can anticipate and avoid many worst-case scenarios.

TIPS AND ADVICE

Tip: Plan Ahead

Superintendents develop relationships with the community so that communication with key stakeholders can easily occur if a critical issue arises. Good communication with the public helps prevent misunderstanding and misinformation about issues important to the school district. The superintendent who builds positive relationships is in a better position with the public to explain, promote, or inform them of what is needed for the students and why.

Example:

A superintendent had an important school bond campaign coming to the voters. He had spent a great amount of time connecting with various individuals and groups within the community since his arrival in the district five years ago. He had deliberately sought out opportunities to attend civic and community events and meetings for the purpose of talking about the district and its strengths, needs, and priorities. He joined the local Chamber of Commerce and provided regular updates concerning the district's facilities study and other issues facing the district, such as enrollment growth, especially at the elementary level.

The superintendent attended civic events, and often volunteered to be a bell ringer, grill master, food server, driver, holiday light judge, and participant in a variety of events that benefited community residents. Not only did he see the value in doing these things but also he genuinely enjoyed getting to know members of the community in many different venues.

As a result of these efforts, when the time came to create a community task force to support the bond issue, nearly one hundred community residents volunteered. The Executive Board of the Chamber of Commerce also endorsed the bond issue and gave it its support.

In addition, relationships had been established with senior centers and assisted living facilities. Presentations about the schools and district were made on a number of occasions to those groups. When the votes were counted, the highest positive vote occurred in the township with the largest number of senior citizens. It was testimony to the fact that building relationships helped the community better understand (and support) their schools.

While time-consuming, this action by the superintendent was instrumental in garnering the support of the community for the important school bond vote.

Advice:

Building positive school-community relationships is important for many reasons. When the community feels that they are informed and involved in their schools, they are much more likely to provide support when the schools face a critical need. Building relationships also adds to community pride and greater support for the students.

Tip: Plan Well

Some issues are so large that they require as much advance planning as possible. One such example is building a new school. The more lead time available prior to the actual community vote, the better. In these large, complex issues, the more the superintendent anticipates and addresses community questions and concerns, the less likely the superintendent is put in a defensive posture by those who oppose the decision.

Example:

A superintendent was hired in a rapidly growing district. It was obvious that a new elementary school was needed. So, the first order of business was to plan for the building project. Even though it seemed fairly obvious that the district was out of classroom space, nothing was taken for granted. Data on enrollments was gathered. Communication with the city and townships provided access to information on new housing developments, land purchases, and plans for possible new roads and utilities in the district.

A planning committee was formed that included representatives from schools, governments, businesses, parents, residents, senior citizens, students, school board members, and administration. The committee heard presentations from every academic department in the district (on how increased student population affected their area and what space needs they have for the future), and committee meetings were rotated so they were held at least once in each of the district's schools. A building tour was part of each committee meeting agenda. Committee members may or may not have had knowledge of the district's schools, so the tours helped familiarize them with the facilities and potential space issues.

The superintendent developed a Request for Proposal for architect services and one for construction management services. The board developed selection criteria, screened responses, interviewed finalists, and selected the architect and construction management firm. Once recommendations were made from the larger committee about the size of the new school and additions to some other facilities, a smaller committee was formed. That committee met with the newly selected architect firm to review concept drawings of the new school. Estimates were assigned to each of five options. The committee selected the two options they believed best met the needs of the students and the budget. The school board then met in three different work-study sessions to review and discuss various aspects of the two options. The school board made formal decisions regarding the new building appearance, size, cost, and determined size and location of additions to existing buildings.

With the building plan selected, public presentations were held in each community in the district. As per law, detailed documents were developed and sent to every taxpayer, and a Frequently Asked Questions section summarized main points. The local paper editorial board was approached and asked to publicly support the issue (which they did). The vote was successful. The new school was built and ready to open on time and under budget. The planning process was detailed well ahead of the actual activities. The superintendent understood that this complex issue required a written, well-developed plan.

Advice:

The more detailed the planning effort around large and complex issues, the better. Plan well, involve key stakeholders, and structure the input from the stakeholders so that it is meaningful and used. Anticipate questions and concerns and address those as soon as possible.

Tip: Anticipate Test Score Interest

Test scores are an important topic in all school districts. How well students perform is viewed as a key indicator of the quality of the schools. A superintendent, or his/her subordinate administrator, anticipates questions that may be asked by the public on the topic of test scores or student achievement. This helps develop achievement data information that is meaningful and important to parents and the school community.

Example:

Most states have designated times of the year that tests are given to students in various grades and in various subjects. The achievement reports for each school and district are made public by both the media and the school district. Most superintendents realize that achievement results are not theirs to either criticize or brag about. Their role is to assure that factual information is reported with some interpretation of the overall results. If a superintendent takes credit for student achievement (or overemphasizes test results), then he/she takes the blame when the student achievement levels go down.

The most practical response to test-score mania is to identify what is important to report to the parents and the school community. Students achieve milestones that are not test related. These are just as important to report to the public as are scores on a standardized test. By anticipating the public's need to hear how students are doing, superintendents can structure the creation of a variety of presentations and information documents to keep the public aware of student successes.

In one large, suburban district, the superintendent scheduled a student presentation at each school board meeting. The presentations were student led and always featured an activity in which students had pride of accomplishment. Since the board meetings were televised, the student presentations were viewed by thousands of people. The superintendent scheduled the presentations by communicating with the administrative team in the spring and fall to make sure they each had at least one student-led presentation at every board meeting. Students were apprised ahead of time of the proper protocol for presenting to the school board.

The public was made aware of many student accomplishments throughout the year. Test scores were also discussed and reported, but the superintendent in this suburban district addressed the need to report achievement data by creating his own method. Showcasing students and their accomplishments became a much-anticipated part of the school board meeting.

Advice:

Educational organizations are accountable to the public. Because of this fact, the public requests (and sometimes demands) information about progress in educating children. The superintendent can anticipate what the public wants to know and can provide structured, planned information that demonstrates both factual academic progress and student accomplishments.

Tip: Tell the Truth—Always

Never tell a half truth or nontruth to the public even on the small issues. Always anticipate that the truth will eventually be known. Once a lie is exposed, the trust that a superintendent has developed with the community up to that point in time can be destroyed—maybe never to return again.

Example:

The superintendent of a large metropolitan school district was in her second year of tenure with the district. She came from outside of the system and in fact, from outside of the state. The school board was pleased with their selection, and the school community was beginning to be acclimated to her leadership and her style. Although some thought she might be a touch aloof, others saw her as more of a shy, intelligent person who was easy to approach.

The district in which she served was diverse in wealth, race, and ethnicity. A few problems had surfaced in recent years with some gang-related activity at one of three high schools. One of the high schools also had a past event that resulted in a student being attacked viciously on school property. Even given these situations, the district did enjoy a positive reputation for student athletic and academic achievement.

One morning in early fall, the radio and television stations reported that one of the high schools in that district would not hold class that day due to a water leak. Students were advised, in many messages starting around 5:30 a.m., to not attend class due to the water leak.

The next morning, the newspapers, radio, and television stations carried the breaking news that there was no water leak at the high school as reported the day before. The truth was that at the end of the school day (the day before) some students heard about a student who made a threat to do something violent the next day at school. They reported it to the principal. Because the apparent threat was for the next day, the superintendent decided to call off school for that day. But she did not want to state the real reason, saying later that she thought if she told the reason publicly, it would impede the investigation into who made the threat. So, she made up the story of the water leak.

Many radio stations spent a great deal of time on this—discussing whether lying to the students and the public was the right thing to do or not. The superintendent did not anticipate that her decision to lie about the reason for school being cancelled (even though she thought she had a good rationale) would have such widespread and negative consequences. Even close colleagues were somewhat stunned. Telling the truth is always the right (and only) thing to do.

Advice:

Always think—What is the worst thing that can happen if I do this? Also, since there is usually more than one "right" decision for most situations, the one that maintains the trust and integrity of the position and the person is the one to pick.

Tip: Put Yourself in Another's Shoes

It is best not to assume that well-intended actions by students always have a positive outcome. Even good intentions can sometimes escalate into a large, negative result.

Example:

Three high school students, who were student editors of the yearbook, wanted to acknowledge the fiftieth-year anniversary of their school. Part of their proposed celebration included placing the school's original Indian Chief Logo on the front of the yearbook—a logo that had been changed many years ago out of respect for the Native American population in the district. The new logo was a tiger and had been the logo/mascot for twenty years. The principal of the large high school questioned the appropriateness of such an action and said no to the students and the yearbook sponsor. They asked to go up the chain of command and ended up meeting with the superintendent. They explained their rationale that using the old logo acknowledged the history of the school and they wanted to celebrate, one more time, the old logo.

The superintendent listened carefully and said that he did not think it was a good idea and agreed with the principal. He thought the use of the logo would be offensive to the district's Native American residents. The superintendent said that he would meet with the Indian Committee members at one of their regularly scheduled meetings and ask them how they felt about the issue. He said he would communicate their response back to the students and principal.

The superintendent did meet with the members of the Indian Committee (that is the official name of the committee). They appreciated the fact that they were asked about the issue. All of them shared the same opinion: they did not want the logo on the cover of the yearbook, nor did they want it used at all. They said they found it offensive and offered to speak with the students if the superintendent felt it would be helpful.

The superintendent took the message back to the students and the principal. He suggested that the students should meet with the committee members.

The students did not feel that was necessary. They were surprised, however, with the Indian Committee member reaction because they truly did not see how their idea about the logo could be viewed as offensive. But the students respected the wishes of the Indian Committee members.

Because the principal and the superintendent both anticipated a possible negative reaction to the proposed student action, they followed up and avoided a potentially harmful breach in friendship and support from the Native American community.

Advice:

Students learn lessons from many people in their school career. Not all of the lessons come from teachers. Superintendents seek ways to help students broaden their perspectives and find the teachable moments in some of the most unexpected places. Anticipate outcomes of even well-intended actions.

Tip: Know When to Seek Legal Counsel

Superintendents understand that litigation is part of the business of operating a school system. No school district is immune from grievances or lawsuits. Astute administrators, always vigilant regarding possible legal involvement, keep excellent records of contacts with individuals who have concerns or displeasure with the district, its policies, procedures, or practices.

Example:

Superintendents seem to develop, with time and experience, a sixth sense for when an issue may escalate into something that requires advice or counsel from school district attorneys. Personnel issues seem to take an inordinate amount of time to address and have a likelihood of ending up requiring the services of the school district's attorney. For example, in a midsized suburban district, the superintendent received a call from the local police chief. The chief told the superintendent that he received information about a possible drug-related theft in another community and someone in the district may be involved.

The person being held and investigated for the theft was a resident in the local community and was a district teacher. Both the police chief and the superintendent knew the person well. The superintendent called the building principal and met with him within the hour. In their discussion, the principal revealed that several staff in his building recently had items stolen from their purses or desks. Nothing was substantial, and it amounted mostly to a few dollars. The principal thought the thefts were the work of "volunteers" in the building who had not had background checks. He did not for a minute suspect that the teacher was involved. But, given the circumstances, he felt that perhaps there was a possibility that the teacher was somehow involved because apparently the alleged theft was for money to purchase drugs.

Because the teacher was being held in a community very far from the local area, it was unlikely that the information about the theft would find its way to the local community very soon. As would be expected, the tearful teacher soon called the principal. The superintendent and principal arranged to meet her in an out-of-town location. The superintendent, in the meantime, contacted legal counsel in anticipation of the meeting and asked whether there was justification to ask for a resignation before the charges were "official." The meeting took place. After some discussion, the superintendent provided the option to the teacher of a voluntary resignation with the understanding that confidentiality from the district would be maintained if at all possible.

The superintendent asked if the teacher thought about seeking counseling and drug treatment. The teacher admitted being addicted to cocaine and was embarrassed to say that it was her husband who first introduced her to the drug. She had left him but was struggling with her addiction and with her finances.

The teacher sent a letter of resignation the next day. She also admitted herself to a treatment facility. The courts were fairly lenient regarding her arrest. Not many people in the school or district knew why the teacher resigned, and that was the way it stayed.

Advice:

Seek legal counsel before it is needed—not during or after—if at all possible. Plan for the worst but be grateful for the best in a difficult situation.

Chapter Eight

Facilitating Meaningful Change

Even the most experienced, successful superintendents would agree that leading a change process can be difficult at best, and expensive and unproductive at worst. The old saying "if it isn't broken, don't fix it" reflects the attitude of some members within and outside of the school community. Part of the challenge of facilitating change is to convince (inspire) people that the "new" or different approach is worth the time, energy, and resource investment. Even when the merits are clear, barriers to success are part of the change process.

If the superintendent forces change (top-down style of leadership), then those affected may feel they have little or no control over their work environment. Forced change may be done for the right reasons, but the resulting impact on employee morale can undermine implementation.

Even when change is grass roots, a lack of preparation, limited resources, or not enough implementation time can lead to premature abandonment of the change. Future change efforts will receive little enthusiasm if past efforts are not successful.

When staff experience frequent turnover in superintendents, they may adopt an attitude, legitimately, of indifference to change efforts coming out of the superintendent's office. What they have learned is, given enough time, the change initiative will disappear, just like the superintendent.

When facilitating meaningful change, the operative word is meaningful. Fullan (2007) states, "The problem of meaning is central to making sense of educational change" (p. 8). Fullan (2007) also discusses the importance of understanding how change affects the individual as well as how change is a process occurring within a much larger social and political context. Those who facilitate change understand that for greatest success, change should make sense, be grounded in purpose, and detail not only what needs to be done but also how.

PREPARE FOR RESISTANCE

Superintendents who approach the change process as logical, necessary, and supported by good data may soon discover that the resistance
to change comes from an emotional reaction by subordinate staff rather
than a professional one. Common questions raised by those affected by
the change process are: Will I be as successful as I am now? What if I am
the only one who cannot adapt? Will the change really be worth my time
and effort? Why do I need to change—am I not performing well enough?
Will those affected respond positively to something new? Will it really be
better? Is this just another fad? Fear of failure and fear of the unknown
are powerful disincentives to change. The emotional reaction to change
is real and influences receptivity to changing anything, even if relatively
insignificant.

It is wise for a new superintendent to gather information regarding the history of change initiatives in the district. A review of how those were planned,
organized, and implemented may provide insight into the attitude of district
staff and patrons toward any discussion about a new direction, program, or
goal.

Most change is driven by the identification of a problem or issue that, if
addressed, results in greater return than if left alone. Teachers and administrators continually develop new or modified instructional strategies in
their classroom or school because they believe those better serve students.
The fact is, change occurs all the time in education. There is no shortage of
issues that benefit from "tweaking." But those engaged in modifying or improving their work may not actually call the process of doing so "change."
Even the phrase *continuous improvement* may evoke a negative reaction
because it may be interpreted as "I am not performing well enough so I have
to improve." How people "feel" about the need to change certainly affects
their will to change.

Superintendents find that the development of a strategic plan can provide
a calming influence for staff, parents, and even the school board. The large-
and small-group discussions around district strengths, weaknesses, and highest priority needs help focus attention on goal setting and action planning.
In many instances, the plan details what needs to change and how. It also
provides direction for allocation of resources, time lines, and staff development to accomplish the specified goals. When there is a process for changing
or improving the educational program for students, and those improvements
make sense to people, their reaction to change is usually much more positive.
The fear of change is minimized because the mystery of what is going to happen in the change is eliminated.

VIEW CHANGE AS A PLANNING PROCESS

Some may argue that change is an event; others that it is a journey. What it is not is arbitrary. Change requires planning. Planning is the anticipation (and study) of current and future needs of students and the organization. Successful and experienced superintendents focus time, energy, and resources on issues that have the greatest impact on what students need and what the organization can sustain. Deliberate and strategic planning identifies specific, measureable goals that in turn drive resources, time, and energy on these predetermined areas of need.

Superintendents who plan well gather and analyze student and organization data. They know the district's demographics and traditions, anticipate future issues, and facilitate targeted initiatives rather than sweeping reforms. They seek information from administrators, staff, parents, and the school board on district strengths, weaknesses, and highest priorities. They seldom veer from the plan and keep the goals in the forefront of discussion with administrators and staff. They share the goals with their community and report on progress. Change for them is the result of a planning process, not a whim.

Astute superintendents avoid imposing immediate, top-down change initiatives as soon as they are hired. Similarly, they avoid changing their new district's policies, practices, and procedures to match those of their previous district. Although some of those changes may be valuable and perhaps even needed, the planning process requires that the culture, traditions, strengths, needs, and priorities of their current district provide the foundation for any change efforts. Ownership in the change is a critical step in planning for change. Change for change sake does not provide opportunity for ownership.

Experienced superintendents understand that time spent trying to convince people to embrace change is not as effective as identifying personnel willing to take a lead role in the change process. The people who are positive and see how the change can benefit students are the very people that need to be involved in leadership roles within the school district. Committees and task forces formed to study and plan for change are more effective and productive if led by teachers and administrators who see the change as needed, focused, and beneficial to the students.

STUDY EXPERT ADVICE

Experts on the topic of organizational change have written volumes about proper process, approach, conditions, preparation, and strategies to lead change. Burke, Smith, Fullan, Kotter, and among many experts on the subject, provide research, insights, and recommendations that every prospective superintendent should study and understand. Burke (2008) states, "Organizations change all the time, each and every day. The change that occurs in organizations is, for the most part, unplanned and gradual" (p. 1).

Smith (2008) refers to how change disrupts our routines, challenges our assumptions, creates stress, leads to resistance, and can result in unpredictable and even unintended consequences. Fullan (2001) believes that those who lead with a moral purpose, understand change, attend to relationships, increase knowledge within the organization, and seek coherence are more successful in leading in a changing, dynamic culture than those who don't. Kotter's (1996) eight-stage process of creating major change is grounded in addressing the barriers and errors common to organizational change efforts and their consequences.

The more a superintendent studies organizational change, the more he/she acquires the skills necessary to know what must happen to make the organization more effective and efficient and what must be done to assure the mission and vision of the organization is realized.

RECOGNIZE THE PURPOSE OF CHANGE

Good enough is not good enough anymore (Collins, 2001). The public expects and requires better, improved educational methods, materials, and technologies in schools. Additionally, these improved strategies must be implemented faster and with fewer resources—both material and personnel—in classrooms today. Drucker (1999) said that organizations have to view change as the norm and be designed for change. Organizations must create change, not react to it. Effective leaders take charge of the purpose of change and talk about the necessity of change. Once they do so, they facilitate and inspire others to think creatively, deliberately, and proactively to better meet the needs of all students. It is up to the superintendent to communicate with stakeholders what is important in the district and the school community.

If change is needed to meet the goals that are important to accomplish in the district, then that is what the superintendent must talk about with staff, students, parents, community members, and the school board. The superintendent lets the school community know the purpose of change because understanding why the change is needed is as important as the implementation process itself. Meaningful change is the only change that is sustainable in the culture of the organization.

AVOID "ONE SIZE FITS ALL" REFORMS

New superintendents may be tempted to embrace the most current new reform efforts or practice in education. Leaders, just like most of us, do not want to be left out of the attention given to a new idea, specifically if everyone is adopting it. After all, what if it really is the best idea around and the district is not on board? Superintendents, though, know that the new idea may not work as well in every district. Because districts differ significantly in demographics, traditions, culture, and student achievement, not all practices (reforms) are appropriate for every district. Superintendents evaluate new practices, policies, and initiatives in terms of fit for students and the school community. In tough financial times, it is vital that resources are aligned to educational goals based on student priorities, not on pressure to conform. The new idea may actually be appropriate, but that is determined after it has been weighed and measured against the district's highest priority needs for its students.

PREPARE STAFF

A critical step in implementing any change, large or small, is to make sure staff and students are prepared. Whether implementing something new or modifying existing programs and delivery, planned change requires staff development, communication with stakeholders, and examination of what, if anything, will be modified or eliminated as a result of the change. Some excellent ideas have failed because the staff members are not properly prepared for how their work will be different. If they are not well prepared, successful implementation is not likely. Preparing staff for change is an integral component of the planning process.

EVALUATE RESULTS

Once change is planned, organized, and implemented, the results must be evaluated. This evaluation is needed to determine how effective the initiative has been in meeting original goals and whether the change made the desired impact on student learning. Because schools have such limited resources, it is more important than ever to know if the new ideas, programs, services, or materials have been worth the investment.

As mentioned before, change is not an arbitrary activity based on the hope that some improvement occurs. It is a planned, meaningful process based on data, goals, and evaluation. The results of evaluations are reported to those vested in the change and, often, to the greater school community. The evaluation step is essential in a time of limited resources and system accountability.

KEEP THE FOCUS

Planning, organizing, preparing, implementing, evaluating, and reporting are the steps used to approach change within the organization. But the work of monitoring, evaluating, and improving effectiveness and efficiency in the organization never stops. In other words, change is the norm; it is conceptually imbedded in any successful organization. Therefore, the superintendent is required to keep the focus on the plans for improvement, on the goals that reflect the mission of the organization. He/she does this by:

- Presenting to the school board on progress toward meeting goals
- Garnering administrator support
- Communicating with the public regarding district priorities
- Promoting meaningful staff development
- Allocating resources to important goals
- Developing new and updated goals
- Using implementation time lines
- Evaluating policies, practices, procedures
- Reporting to stakeholders
- Gathering and analyzing data
- Engaging in cost-benefit analysis of practices
- Conducting annual evaluation of goals, activities, and time lines

ESSENCE OF FACILITATING MEANINGFUL CHANGE

Change is a process that focuses resources on planned goals designed to assure that all students achieve the greatest success in the educational environment. Time devoted to discussions about the "need to change" is better spent on using meaningful data to identify highest priority programs, services, materials, equipment, and instructional methodologies needed to assure student success. Superintendents who understand and mitigate the emotional impact of change are better facilitators of the change process.

TIPS AND ADVICE

Tip: Involve Others in Change

Change may be logical and reasonable yet not accepted if those affected by the change have not had sufficient involvement in planning the change.

Example:

A superintendent was contacted in the fall of the year by three elementary teachers who wanted to meet to discuss concerns they had about the building principal. When asked if they had discussed these concerns with their principal, they said yes, but they received no satisfactory response from him. The superintendent contacted the principal and said that he was going to set a meeting with some of the teachers from his building and asked the principal for any insight he had into the situation.

In the meeting with the superintendent, teachers said that they were tired of the principal's authoritarian, "my way or the highway" attitude. The principal had served in the elementary school for twelve years, and his leadership had met with some complaints from staff over the years, but nothing like the most recent barrage. The teachers brought some documentation regarding a number of issues to the meeting. Their main concern was that the principal had planned a literacy goal for the building over the summer and now, in the fall, everyone in the building had to get on board with his plan. The teachers said that members of the literacy committee were not apprised of the new goal and that even the language arts committee members were not involved—except for two of the principal's favorite teachers.

The superintendent quickly determined that several problems were wrapped into the complaint. These were:

- Lack of communication over the summer by the principal with the two established building committees
- An assumption made by the principal that the data he presented on student achievement results at a spring staff meeting were sufficient to justify the change
- Not all in-service plans for the year were able to include all staff—some had to wait for training for two years
- No paraprofessional staff members were included in the plans for training
- Staff were suspect of how committee members were selected by the principal

The superintendent had three meetings with staff and many meetings with the principal. All sides were defensive regarding their opinions. The superintendent concluded that the intentions of the principal were honorable and that concerns brought forward by the staff had some merit.

The superintendent provided the principal with specific activities to try to rebuild trust and communication with staff. These were implemented, but a handful of staff members were not receptive to the efforts. It was also determined that the committee structure needed to be revised and the staff needed to have greater involvement in planning building goals.

Advice:

Change, particularly change that affects an entire staff, must follow a process that is inclusive and clear to everyone. Not all may agree with the change and some may resist the change, but if they have had the chance to voice their opinion, the process produces less friction.

Tip: Sometimes a New Idea Needs To Be Field Tested

School board meetings should be as efficient as possible, but the school board may resist changing a procedure they have used for years at the board table. Field testing an idea may be helpful to ease into a new procedure.

Example:

A new superintendent took the advice of a veteran superintendent, who told her to hold a work-study session with the school board as soon as possible into her tenure to discuss operating principles. The work-study session was scheduled a week-and-a-half into the new superintendent's tenure. It is important to note that the new superintendent had been an assistant superintendent in a large metropolitan district much different in size, culture, and location than her new district. Even before she officially started her job in the new district, the superintendent attended several school board meetings to observe the interaction between the school board members and the previous superintendent.

The session went well, with the agenda covering role and operation expectations between the school board and the superintendent. Other items covered included school board meeting protocol, agenda format, Robert's Rules of Order, role of the school board chair, public forum, audience interaction, board presentations, and a few other detail items. Because the superintendent had observed that the school board meeting was very informal and somewhat chaotic, she brought up an idea for adding formality to the meeting. She suggested two things: each board member should signal the board chair (raise a hand, leaving the elbow on the table), and board members should refrain from talking to the audience during the board meeting.

The school board was OK with not talking to the audience during the meeting, but they were hesitant to accept the idea that they should raise their hand to speak. They thought it might inhibit board member conversations. They said they would try it for three months to see if it worked better than their system of just talking when they wanted to. At the end of three months, they officially adopted the hand-up procedure as one to be used at every board meeting by all board members.

Adding formality to a school board meeting was a challenge for this board. But they found that this particular formality did make the meeting flow better and allowed each member to talk without being interrupted.

Advice:

New superintendents need to be careful about being critical of their new school board and how they run their business, but a work-study session on operating principles provides an opportunity to talk about trying new procedures that may actually work better than the old ones.

Tip: Avoid Pressure to Act Too Quickly

A new superintendent may find that his or her school board has been waiting until he/she is officially on board before indicating they want to change something. Usually the previous superintendent either did not agree with the change or was part of the problem. These are often sensitive issues that need study and analysis before the new superintendent can commit to whatever the change it is that the school board is seeking.

Example:

A new superintendent was excited to have obtained his first position in a small but viable district. The school board was also pleased with their selection and voted unanimously to hire their first choice of candidate. The new superintendent was a former high school principal in another district, quite a distance from the current district.

About two weeks into his tenure as a superintendent, the school board chair asked to meet with him on an item of importance. When they met, the board chair told the superintendent that the school board was united in a decision that the high school principal should be fired.

This was news to the new superintendent, and it took him by surprise. Initially, he was not sure how to respond to the school board chair and just listened without saying much at all. The new superintendent contacted a trusted colleague superintendent. He explained the situation. The two arranged to meet but not in either of their school districts, for confidentiality reasons.

The more experienced superintendent advised his colleague to meet with the school board chair to explain that "firing an administrator" is a legal procedure and that the person involved has due process rights. If due process is violated, the school board and district could be placed in an undesirable situation—one that certainly would become public. He suggested that the new superintendent explain that one of the responsibilities of the superintendent is to evaluate administrative staff and that responsibility is taken very seriously.

The new superintendent set a meeting with the school board chair to discuss the issues brought up in the conversation he had with his colleague. Before that meeting, he had contacted the school district attorney to clarify procedures for employee termination. He also obtained copies of his state's statute that covered termination. Armed with this information, the superintendent explained the legal issues related to the situation, and he clarified that it is his responsibility to conduct performance reviews of district administrators.

This meeting did help relieve the pressure the superintendent had felt from the board chair. She saw that it was in the best interest of the district to follow the processes outlined by the superintendent.

The new superintendent evaluated the principal's performance as part of his job responsibility. Where needed, improvement goals were identified. The principal eventually left the district, but there was no tumultuous event associated with the change.

When board members want immediate change, a superintendent must have the courage to do the right thing and to protect the district and school board from avoidable legal issues.

Advice:

Stay the course even when pressure is on. Implementing a change for the wrong reasons and abandoning proper planning practices almost always lead to disastrous results.

Tip: Needed Change May Not Be Desired Change

Limited resources can force change that is neither desired nor positive for students. A superintendent must be responsible for decisions that change the way a district conducts business. Some of those decisions go against best practices in educating students but must be done to keep the school open and teachers in the classroom.

Example:

The superintendent of a district of about 550 students knew that it was only a matter of time before the district would be forced to dissolve or consolidate. Enrollments were declining, and enrollment projections showed that trend would continue. The superintendent began discussion among parents and district residents about the situation and the reality of what declining enrollment would mean.

In this informal discussion, he tried to determine how the residents would react to consolidating with a neighboring district. As he expected, the receptivity to consolidation was almost zero. As the superintendent explored options and developed scenarios for the future, one idea emerged as a temporary but viable option. That idea was to change the traditional five-day school week to a four-day school week. The district could preserve and protect its classroom teachers for one more year before being forced to close its doors if that idea was implemented.

The superintendent found, through his study of the issue, that his district could save $62,000 a year by implementing a four-day school week. The savings were almost entirely from transportation expenses.

He provided forums for discussion about this change and invited local media to feature information he provided to them about how the four-day week operates. Interestingly, the superintendent did not think the four-day week had any educational benefit for students, and in fact, he firmly believed that more time in school, longer days and more of them, were needed to help assure that all children would have the opportunity to learn. So this was not something he could sell to the public for any other reason than in his mind it would save money.

The board voted, and the four-day week was implemented. The public reaction was minimal. At the end of the first year of this major change, the district was forced to dissolve—much like the superintendent had predicted.

Advice:

Facilitating change sometimes means determining the best course of action in the worst of conditions.

Tip: Vision Statements Are More than Just Words

The purpose of a vision is not to create a lofty-sounding statement to be put on letterhead but rather to provide direction to members of the school community in their work and interaction with students. Policies, practices, and procedures are constantly reviewed and modified to support the goals of the district based on the vision.

Example:

The superintendent believed that one of the most significant challenges for a superintendent in the systemic change process is to get full buy-in and understanding of the educational needs of the organization from the finance department/director. In his district, the new superintendent made sure that the finance director and the associate superintendent for business operations were completely engaged in strategy sessions to determine the five-year strategic plan. The associate superintendent was highly capable but was, like the superintendent, a newcomer to the district. The finance director, however, was a native of the city and a veteran employee of the district.

As part of the long-range plan, the superintendent, with support from the associate superintendent, delegated the design and implementation of a site-based budgeting process to the finance director. This process involved the removal of authority and accountability for funding distribution from the central office administrators and, instead, placed the responsibility for building funding decisions directly in the hands of the principals.

The finance director was a highly skilled CPA with deep knowledge and experience in banking, auditing, and accounting. The superintendent wanted this type of expertise in the design of the site-based budgeting process, yet he was sensitive to the educational context of work that needed to be done. The superintendent, rather than directing how this critical change should be done, used the vision of the organization to create the context for the change. The vision provided the basis for understanding and commitment from the finance director, district administrators, and principals. The vision helped drive dramatic and incremental change at every level. The superintendent's time investment with the finance director on the vision of the organization was well spent.

With the help of the superintendent and associate superintendent, the finance director designed and successfully implemented one of the first site-based budgeting processes in the nation. And, because she understood and was committed to the organizational vision, the finance director became one of the superintendent's most loyal and capable administrators in the district.

Advice:

Sometimes it is essential to go slowly in order to move quickly. The time invested in building the capacity of leaders so they understand why major changes need to occur is often the difference between change that is systemic and sustainable and change that is unfocused and temporary.

Chapter Nine

Advocating for Students

Superintendents expect and want to be student advocates. This advocacy is primarily accomplished by the superintendent's belief in and focus on the school district's mission, assuring all students have the opportunity to succeed as learners. School boards that seek a new superintendent may specifically mention this quality of leadership—advocacy for all students—in the position profile. However, there is some debate as to whether it is essential for a superintendent to come from the educator ranks in order to be a student advocate (Kowalski, 2006).

Whether from the educator ranks or not, the superintendent who keeps the organization focused on the district mission positively affects the learning environment for students. Through hiring practices, strategic planning goals, school board relationships, policy development, and community connections, the superintendent influences the quality of education for each student.

REVIEW THE DISTRICT PLAN

Reviewing, refining, and updating the district strategic plan is an important responsibility for a superintendent. It often is one of the first tasks on a new superintendent's to-do list. The plan informs the superintendent about what the stakeholders in the school community have identified as the highest priority issues to be addressed to accomplish the district's mission. The review process allows the superintendent to evaluate each goal to determine whether it is too general to make a meaningful difference to students or too specific, looking more like an action step than a guiding principle. For example, the superintendent may judge the goal "to increase student achievement" as too general and, in his or her review of the plan, find that the more appropriate goal would be "to raise student achievement in reading in the primary grades."

Sometimes the superintendent may find that the goals of the existing plan are specific enough, but that there are too many. Too many goals dilute the overall plan. A focused plan with few goals directs energy, resources, and time to the highest priorities. The superintendent may feel it is necessary to bring a planning group together to assist in the review of the existing plan. This group, with the superintendent, examines the goal statements, action plans, time lines, and identified resources. The group then offers recommendations for plan modifications or, perhaps, a complete overhaul of the plan.

For superintendents who work well with strategic goals and a focused direction, this planning process is critical to student advocacy.

GATHER, ANALYZE, AND USE MEANINGFUL DATA

"Within the current policy environment, one of the most widespread reasons that data-based decisions making is so important for school leaders is to meet accountability requirements" (Guthrie and Schuermann, 2010, p. 266). In other words, there is an expectation that superintendents focus on all students, their achievements, and their successes. This charge and challenge requires gathering, analyzing, and using important, meaningful data. The data gathered should be disaggregated to gain information on how well students are performing by age, gender, race, ethnicity, socioeconomic status, and a myriad of other categories. This helps to evaluate and determine which programs and services best serve the district's students—by individual students' needs as well as by select groups.

In order to access meaningful data for instruction and overall organizational improvement (Data Management and Analysis or DMA), technology advancements are used to connect "… student data, attendance, discipline, scheduling, assessment, teacher evaluation, budgeting, accounting, purchasing, employee records, and other administrative systems" (Cunningham and Cordeiro, 2009, p. 85). This connection of data produces conclusions, trends, summaries, and specific information that lead educators to what needs to be addressed and, in some instances, how. For example, if the student attendance data show that students who fail to graduate often have the poorest attendance record, then this connection illustrates something very important for the high school staff to address. They also know that the importance of attendance needs to become a priority issue among staff, parents, and the students themselves.

Data provide a picture of what seems to be working, what could be eliminated as ineffective, and what should be added or revised to impact student success. For example, data on first grade reading scores show a marked and sustained increase for a two-year time period. Investigation into what changed, if anything, two years ago found that thirty more minutes of direct reading instruction was added to the first grade curriculum at that time. The conclusion would be that more time spent on reading led to greater student achievement. Therefore, the thirty minutes of direct reading instruction should be continued, and perhaps increased. Additional years of tracking progress will provide meaningful trend data.

MAKE THE BEST HIRING DECISIONS

To advocate for students, it is important that the superintendent have the right people in positions that have greatest influence on student achievement and success. Principals are instrumental in creating an educational environment that supports quality and effective programs and services for all students. Successful superintendents search for principals who are educational leaders, who understand the teaching-learning process, and know how data is used to improve curriculum and instruction to best meet the student achievement goals.

Charlotte Danielson (2002) discusses the importance of administrators understanding the nuances of school improvement efforts. She concurs with those who believe that without this understanding by school leaders of effective instructional practices and professional community building, school reform efforts consistently fail. Superintendents must hire administrators who demonstrate the knowledge and understanding of school improvement efforts.

Prior to reviewing applicant files and interviewing candidates for a principal position, superintendents identify selection criteria based on the skills, abilities, and dispositions required for the open position. These often include:

- Belief in planning to achieve priority goals
- Knowledge about program improvement
- Ability to assess excellence in teaching
- Ability to communicate well with staff, parents, students, and the school community
- Ability to articulate the importance of curriculum review, instructional methodologies, and assessment in program improvement
- Courage to make the right decision for the right reasons
- Belief that being a leader means being a role model
- Passion for education and students
- Belief that all students can learn
- Ability to hire the right staff for the school and classroom

The last point is particularly important. Advocating for students occurs first and foremost in the classroom. Hoy and Hoy (2009) state, "Increasingly the research suggests that the key to improving student learning rests with what happens in the classroom. The teacher is critical" (p. 3).

Because what happens in the classroom is so important, principals not only must know how to select the most qualified teacher but also they must have the courage to retain only the teachers who can demonstrate excellence in teaching.

Superintendents set the expectations for their principals in hiring and retaining the very best classroom teachers. And, to assure the best teachers are retained, performance review is important. Performance review allows for identification of areas for improvement, reinforcement of areas of strength, and discussion of progress toward professional development goals. This does not just apply to principals and their review of their staff; it also applies to the superintendent in his/her annual review of principal performance.

Superintendents who emphasize the importance of hiring the right people know that the students are the benefactors. Student success is the result of highly qualified educators who are passionate about education, work toward common goals, and want all students to succeed.

ASSURE THAT PROFESSIONAL
DEVELOPMENT IS A PRIORITY

Advocating for students cannot occur systemwide if the adults who work in an educational setting do not understand how their behavior, attitude, beliefs, and job performance affect students individually and collectively. Helping staff be successful in their work and in their understanding of the organization's goals and expectations is dependent upon the quality of professional/staff development. Without specific discussion about the mission of the school and the expectations for the employees in achieving the mission, some employees may not see the connection between their work and the larger educational environment. Whether licensed or nonlicensed, this connection should be talked about and reinforced by principals, supervisors, and the superintendent.

When a culture of learning exists within the organization, students benefit. Professional Learning Communities (PLCs) are found in many, if not most, schools today. These PLCs are instrumental in reinforcing the goals set by the school and, often, the district. They provide a support network for participants to advance learning in meaningful ways, ways that directly influence their work with students.

The culture of learning is further reinforced by clearly defined performance standards for employees. When performance expectations are clear, the staff targets professional development opportunities that tie directly to one or more of their duties. Their learning is meaningful. Workplace stress is reduced because employees know what is expected of them as they perform their job.

A culture of learning also provides:

- new employee orientation to the organization's mission
- opportunities to improve job performance
- recognition of excellence in meeting performance standards
- mentorship activities and support
- emphasis on goal setting, action planning, and measurement of progress
- focus on effectiveness, efficiency, and job improvement

To truly advocate for students, the adults within the system know their duties and responsibilities and they have the skills and abilities to perform their work with confidence.

SPEAK UP IN THE POLITICAL ARENA

Superintendents today find themselves increasingly thrust into the political arena to advocate for their students and for children in general. Many superintendents spend time and energy encouraging or dissuading legislators from making decisions that have long-term effects on students. Whether the superintendent is prepared or not for the responsibility, working in the political arena is part of a superintendent's role as a student advocate.

Superintendents know they must do more than beat the drum for more funding when discussing education with lawmakers. Rather than just asking for additional financial support, savvy superintendents today focus on other topics for discussion with legislators, topics in which legislators have more interest. These include: accountability, return on investment, and student achievement results. In these discussions, the following points may be helpful:

- Be creative; showcase initiatives that have been successful and should be continued.
- Tell what is working and why; use data and graphs.
- Tell the unique needs of the district.
- Emphasize and show how the district has been accountable with resources.

- Know and talk about the demographics of the district and the array of programs designed to meet student needs.
- Explain the financial impact of serving exceptional students; not just special needs but those with other unique needs (limited English learners, gifted, homeless).
- Use diagrams and charts to explain trend data, revenues, and expenditures.
- Involve knowledgeable teachers and parents in conversations with or presentations to legislators.
- Tell how new money would be used.
- Use press releases to tell about improvements, successes, and what needs to be continued.
- Meet individually with local area legislators; use recent, understandable data to make important points.
- Use talking points—few but powerful.
- Bring legislative platform discussions to the school board for input and possible action.
- Be specific about methods used to reduce expenditures.
- Determine district's highest priority needs and find other districts with similar needs; form a coalition with those districts.
- Suggest reasonable and doable reforms; be creative and innovative.

Given the current political climate, superintendents find that they are continuously fighting for limited resources. Now is the time for new, creative, innovative educational ideas. Advocating for students today requires asking for and using money to dramatically restructure the educational organization. If restructuring ideas are not coming from school leaders, they will come from others who may or may not have the passion, understanding, and knowledge of education, students, and the challenges of educating all learners.

ESSENCE OF ADVOCATING FOR STUDENTS

Whether in the legislature or writing an article for the district newsletter, superintendents advocate for students. To advocate well, it is important to know as much about the district's student population as possible. However, having information is not enough. Making sure the information is used to improve programs and services for all students is the point. Hiring those who can shape the teaching-learning process, use technology as a learning tool, establish the optimal educational environment, and assess program and personnel performance is important to help all students succeed. Preparation, orientation, and development of staff are benefits to all students. The advocacy for students goes beyond the district into the community and the political arena.

TIPS AND ADVICE

Tip: Seek Answers to Problems Affecting Students

A new superintendent should find out how district students perform on required assessments and what programs and services are in place to address academic strengths and needs of students. A new superintendent should also find out what data are gathered, by whom, and how the data are used to improve opportunities for students.

Example:

The data on enrollment in the district indicated to the second-year superintendent that the district was losing about twenty to twenty-five high school students each year for the past four years. Certainly this was a financial issue for the district, since the end-of-the-year enrollment figures consistently indicated a drop in the high school enrollment. But what concerned the superintendent more than the financial impact was the reason why some students left the system.

The size of the school allowed for a wide array of courses and extra- and cocurricular opportunities for students. Virtually all students had access to athletics, fine arts activities, or academic activities. The enrollment at the high school was 850 students in grades nine through twelve, but the superintendent did not view the number of dropouts as an acceptable percentage of the total high school enrollment. The superintendent put this topic on the administrative team agenda for discussion, hoping to gain insight into the trend. This group discussion was helpful and led to the development of a plan of action to stem the student loss each year. The plan contained four main components:

1. Gather trend data over the last five years and disaggregate data to determine any patterns. The goal was to obtain a picture of the type of student who left, what grade level, whether they returned, what credits they still needed when they dropped, what discipline issues they might have had, any counselor notations, and so on.
2. Find out where the students went after they left the high school, and if they attended another school, whether they graduated.

3. Interview randomly selected students who left the school within the last three years to find out reasons why they left.
4. Develop recommendations that would lead to student retention.

The results from the planning process indicated that many of the students who left did so because the high school courses were too difficult, and, by eleventh grade, they knew they could not accumulate the required number of credits to graduate. Most went to an area learning center or to another high school in a neighboring district. A few enrolled in charter schools.

The recommendation resulting from the investigation was to start a school within a school (called SAIL) to serve students who were behind in credits. The program was flexible enough so that students could take one or all of their coursework in the SAIL program. One teacher was hired, one classroom designated, and one part-time aid was provided. The instruction for those taking their course through the program was computer-based instruction.

The year after the program was in place, the end-of-the-year enrollment data showed that only ten students had left the high school—half as many as would be expected. The second year was even more successful in retaining students. The discussion and investigation led to the formation of a program that better met the needs of a certain segment of the high school population.

Advice:

Superintendents can be instrumental in making sure data are gathered and analyzed regarding student performance, enrollment, attendance, and graduation.

Tip: Get the Facts First

New programs and modification of existing programs keep the school system dynamic and meaningful to students. Because of this, it is helpful to occasionally review and evaluate what programs are offered, to whom, and how successful they are in meeting their intended purpose.

Example:

Many teachers and school board members told a new superintendent in a suburban district that district special education costs were excessive and that the district offered a Cadillac program in a district that could ill afford such extravagance. The superintendent was astute about special education programs, services, and student populations.

The superintendent listened to those who said that the special education program and service models were far too generous with assessment, identification, placement, special accommodations, remediation, paraprofessional staffing, materials and resource selections, parent requests, and caseloads for teaching staff. The superintendent used the administrative team meetings to discuss special education program strengths and concerns. The principals were involved with special education staffing and meetings, but none really felt that they had a good handle on all of the nuances of special education processes and programs districtwide. In fact, they admitted they often delegated special education meeting responsibility to the "lead" special education teacher.

The district was served by a special education cooperative and did not have a special education director. For many years, special education teachers had been in charge of the programs and had great latitude in decision making regarding students and their programs. They were dedicated, professional educators. They became somewhat concerned because the superintendent was "looking" into their area of expertise.

The superintendent met with the special education teachers and told them she was putting a task force together to develop a matrix of special education programs and services offered in the district. She told them the truth—she needed to have a better sense of program processes, the students served, and the upcoming issues that should be addressed. She told the teachers that the "in house" and public perception was that the special education model was too costly and too accommodating to teachers, parents, and students.

The program matrix included the number of students served and in which categories, the number of teaching staff by category, the number of support staff assigned to each program, numbers of duplicated and unduplicated counts of students, the number of students assessed each year, the number placed, intervention strategies typically used, and how the service cooperative personnel interact with the district.

The gathering of that information took a year. The task force met quarterly with the superintendent. The matrix was developed, and all of the information requested was put into graph, chart, spreadsheet, or narrative form. One major result was that the principals were asked to take a more active role in special education placements and program decisions.

Other results included: the high school speech articulation numbers were reduced (along with staffing), students who did not qualify for services were taken off the caseload numbers for special education programs, Teacher Assistant Teams were formed at the elementary and middle schools to provide at least two interventions to classroom teachers before students went through assessment for special education, and the special education service collaborative provided a one-day-a-week coordinator to help monitor compliance issues. Students were better served, and teachers were better used in the new process.

Advice:

Before improvements in programs and services can occur for students, the superintendent should determine the effectiveness of the current program and service models.

Tip: Advocating for Students May Involve Only a Few At a Time

The most obvious way to advocate for students is to identify which students are at risk socially, emotionally, and academically. Advocating for students may mean advocating for only a few students at a time because they need the most help.

Example:

The new superintendent in a large suburban district was well aware that the person in the district's Chemical Health Coordinator position was excellent in doing his job. His reputation was stellar in the region. The superintendent felt fortunate to have the person as part of the staff in the district.

When he first arrived in the district, the superintendent met with all teacher leaders or coordinators who played key roles in overseeing programs and services for students outside of the classroom.

In a meeting with the Chemical Health Coordinator, the superintendent asked him to identify the strengths and needs of the Chemical Health program. The coordinator readily talked about the many successful programs in place for students but said the greatest need was a well-defined transition program for students coming out of treatment for chemical addiction. He identified several aspects of a transition program that needed to be implemented but were not in place.

The superintendent asked the coordinator to write up the transition program details, such as what currently was in place and what was needed. The superintendent also wanted to know what barriers existed to implementation of such a plan. The coordinator did the task assigned and provided some possible funding sources to help support the plan he proposed. The plan did involve asking treatment personnel (therapists and/or doctors) to attend an initial transition meeting with school personnel. These individuals needed to be paid for their time if asked by the school to attend a meeting on the student's behalf. This was a barrier for fully developing the transition program in the past.

The superintendent asked the Chemical Health Coordinator to attend an administrative team meeting and bring the information and plan to that group. After some discussion, it was decided that the grant option was feasible and should be pursued. The school board approved the plan and the grant. The district ultimately received funds to sustain the transition program for two years. The program served eighteen students in that two-year time period. These were very at-risk students who would have had extreme difficulty returning to a school setting without support. Even though time, energy, and resources were involved, the superintendent and coordinator saw a need and found a way to help a few students who needed it most. The district picked up the cost of the program after the two-year grant expired.

Advice:

Trust quality staff members to do their job and to identify needs/priorities based on their knowledge of students and program options.

Tip: Evaluate the Effectiveness of All New Programs

Encourage staff to advocate for students and to be creative in their approach to programs and services that help increase student achievement. Remember, though, any new idea or program should mesh well with the strategic plan goals, meet anticipated outcomes/results, and show positive evaluation results.

Example:

In a school district of 14,000 students, there was no shortage of highly qualified staff. The superintendent was aware that the curriculum in his district was well defined, aligned, and articulated from kindergarten to twelfth grade. The curriculum director had been in the district for many years and was well regarded by teachers and administration. Recent student achievement results indicated that students in fourth grade across all schools were not scoring as well as they should be in reading. Because of that, literacy became a strong emphasis districtwide. New ideas were encouraged and investigated.

The curriculum director often discussed the literacy initiative at administrative meetings, and at one of the meetings he said that a group of first grade teachers had heard about a reading program they wanted to implement as part of the focus on literacy. The teachers even wrote a grant that would pay for the program material and training. The curriculum director thought it would be good to try the program, particularly since the teachers were enthused about the program and because they could use the grant money to fund the start-up costs.

The superintendent was not opposed to innovative new ideas and programs to better meet student needs. But when he told the curriculum director that he wanted an executive summary of the new program, the intended outcomes of the program, the target population of the program, an indication of which goals/objectives meet the district's strategic plan, and how the program results are to be evaluated and reported, the curriculum director was somewhat defensive. When the curriculum director told the teachers what the superintendent said, they became even more defensive and even angry.

The superintendent explained to the curriculum director that his intent was not to stop new ideas but to make sure that resources and teacher time were used with specific outcomes in mind. He also explained that just because a neighboring district used the program (which he found out) did not mean that the program was the best fit with the students and existing curriculum in their schools and district. He offered to meet with the teachers to give encouragement and to explain his position on implementing new programs.

It was decided that one school would implement the program. All of the superintendent's conditions were met. An evaluation at the end of the year indicated that the program should be used as a remedial program and offered after school for first grade students who needed a boost with their basic reading skills. It was also concluded that the program was not a substitute for any part of the current reading series and it was not appropriate for good readers, even though the program indicated it was. It did turn out to be valuable for some students, but not as an adoption for first grade curriculum.

Advice:

Keeping the focus on the mission of the school district is vital to advocating for all students. Activities and programs that do not tie directly to strategic goals should not be considered, unless as a highly controlled pilot program.

Tip: Advocating for Students Starts With the Youngest Students in the District

Sometimes the greatest advocacy for all students systemwide can be found in preschool programs. Providing students with the best possible start in their school career is a worthy goal.

Example:

A local senator contacted a superintendent to say that he had a chance to write the district into a $25,000 youth development bill designed to help at-risk students. The senator lived in the school district and was a supporter of the school system. He was also aware that the district was struggling financially and he was trying is some small way to help the district fund or sustain an at-risk youth program. The superintendent asked how much time she had to put a proposal together. The senator said he needed the completed proposal by 2:00 that afternoon—at the state capitol. The superintendent looked at the clock—it was 10 a.m.

The superintendent agreed, but when she hung up the phone, she wondered how in the world she would come up with a meaningful program, supported by staff, and that used the money to benefit as many students as possible. Since time was fleeting, the superintendent thought about what would help students avoid being labeled "at-risk." Her contact with Title I staff and with preschool and kindergarten teachers gave her the idea: the best way to advocate for youth development and reduce at-risk behavior was to target the very youngest of the district's students, kindergarteners. She identified three Title I schools to participate, one as the "control group" and two as the "experimental group." The $25,000 would be used to develop materials to teach prereading skills to kindergarten students. Parents would participate in training sessions on these prereading skills so they could reinforce the skills each week with their child at home. Parents were required to attend eight training sessions. Transportation was provided for parents who needed it. Each session was offered at two different times, one day time and one evening.

The superintendent wrote a draft of the plan and the proposed budget. She asked the Title I lead teacher to come in to her office, review the proposal, and make any suggestions. The proposal was hand delivered at 2:10 at the state capitol. The proposal was funded, the program was designed and implemented, and the results at the end of one year were astounding. At both of the experimental schools, not one child was referred to Title I services for their first grade year. The Title I lead teacher took the program to even greater success districtwide and soon was helping other districts implement the program. It was called Early Access to Success in Education (EASE).

Advice:

Use opportunities given to accomplish the most important, highest priority issue for students. Keep ideas simple and focused.

Chapter Ten

Seeking, Retaining, and Transitioning Positions

According to Glass and Franceschini (2007), an overwhelming majority (85 percent) of respondents believe that the supply of superintendents is not adequate to fill the positions now or in the future. School boards searching for a new superintendent would no doubt agree. Seated superintendents are rigorously recruited by headhunters and school boards hoping to attract candidates for vacant positions. The "revolving door" potential for most superintendent positions is a reality—especially in small or rural systems. Advice on how to seek, retain, or transition is helpful in this climate of short supply and intense recruitment.

UNDERSTAND THE ROLE AND EXPECTATIONS

According to Fullan (2007), a major change in the superintendency since 2000 is the "growing in-your-face presence of accountability and explicit expectations about student achievement" (p. 211). Additionally, No Child Left Behind creates a public focus on failure of schools to meet student achievement standards. The public hears from a variety of sources (politicians, radio, and television personalities) that "public schools are failing." Improvement plans and threats of loss of funding for already strapped school systems keep school leaders on the defensive. It is no wonder that school administrators who are qualified to assume the role of school superintendent are less inclined to do so than a decade ago.

For many parents, district residents, and many school boards, how well students perform on standardized or state tests is directly related to how well the superintendent does his or her job as the school district's Chief Executive

Officer. The impact a superintendent can actually have on test scores is limited but, when student achievement is consistently low, superintendents feel the pressure to "fix it" or move on. Whether it is student achievement results or some other reason, the turnover rate for superintendents is high (three to five years average tenure in a district depending on which study is used).

But there are still courageous administrators who do aspire to the superintendency. For those who have an interest in the position, the number one reason given is because they believe they can improve the teaching and learning experience for students (Glass and Franceschini, 2007). As complex and challenging the position is, the prospect of making a difference to students, staff, parents, and the community is still a noble and attractive incentive for those who seek the superintendency.

School boards vary in what they look for in their leader. Some want a strong change agent with the courage to take on tough issues. Others seek an instructional leader to focus on teaching and learning. Some school boards prefer a manager to maintain existing programs, services, and goals. Others desire a superintendent who is an effective communicator, collaborator, and public relations expert. And many school boards want all of the above.

In addition to seeking a specific leadership "type" in a prospective superintendent, school boards often have differing expectations for the skills and abilities of their new superintendent. Some want a business-oriented person to manage district finances; others prefer a curriculum, instruction, and assessment specialist; yet others seek someone adept at improving the image of schools in their community. Again, many want their superintendent to be skilled in virtually all aspects of leadership.

No matter what style or skills the superintendent brings to the position, it is certain that the ability to resolve conflict, problem solve, and negotiate are all expectations for the position. Because of time-consuming, challenging, and complex responsibilities of the position, new superintendents may quickly discover that "making a difference" may mean resolving conflict that avoids litigation or negative media coverage. Small victories take on new meaning.

Understanding their role and expectations established by the school board helps aspiring superintendents adjust to their new position once hired.

ASSESS THE FIT

The good news about the shortage of superintendents is that there are more opportunities available for prospective candidates. The not-so-good news is that not all of the opportunities are the best fit for the individual or for the school board. Some helpful hints on determining the best fit include:

1. Anticipate the best time for seeking the position. Family considerations are important and may delay a move to another location to take a position. Children still in high school or a spouse whose job is too important to move are factors known prior to application. If these are deal-breakers, then it is unfair to the school board for a candidate to apply for a position if there is no likelihood he/she will accept the position if offered.
2. Research districts of interest. If possible, visit the location prior to application. Read websites, conduct an Internet search of the district, gather information available from state departments, network with others who may have knowledge of the district, and read recent school board minutes.
3. Become familiar with the district's demographics, finances, strategic plan, and student achievement data.
4. Prepare a list of questions to ask the school board or members of interview teams.
5. Arrive prepared for initial interviews with basic knowledge of the district's plan, goals, school names, enrollments, and community size.
6. Avoid speaking specifically and exclusively about your current school system when responding to questions and media interviews. See yourself as a leader of their district, using your past experiences to illustrate points or examples.
7. Determine, if possible, the highest priorities of the district and the immediate expectations of a new superintendent.
8. Talk about values important to your leadership. Be candid rather than elusive about beliefs related to education.
9. Understand that both the candidate and the school board are looking for the best fit. A new superintendent is just as interested in whether he/she wants to be there as the school board is in having him/her come to the district.
10. Pay attention to "gut level" feelings while in the district.
11. Form opinions about working with individual and collective school board members, but remember that those faces may very well change.
12. If not interested, let the board know as soon as possible.

Seeking a superintendency takes time and research. No district is perfect, and most are challenged with one or more major issues. The mix of personalities and the match with skills, knowledge, and beliefs is an important consideration.

ADJUST TO A NEW ROLE

Some people believe the first year in any new position allows for a "honeymoon period." That is not necessarily true for the new superintendent. It is not unusual for a new superintendent to be faced with pressing issues needing immediate attention within days or weeks of being on the job. Some of those are fairly obvious, like the passage of an upcoming vote that was already planned. Others are brought up by the school board after the contract is signed—like changing the high school schedule, immediately. Other issues are simply unanticipated crisis situations involving staff or students. Be prepared to hit the ground running, and don't plan on a "honeymoon" of any length.

In addition to addressing the expected and unexpected issues, a new superintendent finds it beneficial to spend time getting to know school board members, staff, students, parents, and community members. Assessing their perceptions of the district, its strengths and weaknesses, helps form a plan of action for the future. Listening is a valuable and important behavior for the new superintendent.

Many superintendents find that their first year is extremely busy and that seventy-hour workweeks are common. Attending school functions, spending time at civic and governmental meetings, networking with neighboring superintendents, meeting with individual board members, scheduling time for interviewing staff, students, and community members, meetings with administrators and district-level staff, and settling into a new home if in a new location are all very time-consuming and take more than a few months to accomplish. All of these activities occur simultaneously with becoming familiar with how the district functions, addressing day-to-day issues, preparing for school board meetings, working on planned priorities, and most importantly, keeping the school board members informed. But, as tiring as this is, the up-front time investment pays dividends later on.

Adjusting to a new role also means working on relationships. The relationship the superintendent forms with subordinate staff and the connections established with the school board are both critical to effectiveness (and perhaps longevity) of a new superintendent. As mentioned in chapter 1, establishing trust is no easy feat—especially if trust has not been easily given or earned in the school community in the past—for whatever reason. A few helpful strategies to build relationships and work on trust are:

1. Conduct a work-study session with the school board as soon as possible to discuss operating principles, board meeting and committee structures, expectations, and role clarification.
2. Form an administrative team to provide a means of communicating with building- and district-level leaders.
3. Visit schools.
4. Provide district updates at school staff meetings (with principal approval).
5. Let staff know what is valued and what the priorities are for the district under new leadership (building and district administrators should be apprised of these first).

6. Meet with all employee groups at least twice a year.
7. Find ways to connect with students; ask principals the best way to do so.
8. Start learning names of staff.
9. Listen rather than talk; ask clarification questions to better understand issues.
10. Attend various committee meetings already in place (like curriculum and technology).
11. Schedule five to ten minutes of time with groups that meet regularly (parent organizations, booster clubs, professional development activities).
12. Write congratulatory letters to students and staff for their accomplishments.

DEVELOP TRUST

Retaining a position is more complex than adjusting to a new role. Being involved with the school community, establishing trust, and building relationships with the school board cannot guarantee position retention. The school board determines whether a superintendent stays or goes. There is no one thing that a superintendent does that solidifies his/her longevity. As Houston and Eadie (2002) say, "The people populating school boards are likely to be difficult to work with, and so the board savvy superintendent must be a highly accomplished relationship manager" (p. 17). The most difficult school board member may become the superintendent's greatest advocate if a trusting relationship has been developed. But like in any relationship, it takes work to maintain. A turnover in even one board member can change the dynamics of the relationships previously established.

School board member orientation, individual meetings with a new board member (inviting the school board chair to attend as well) to help welcome them and bring them up to speed on current and future issues, communicating well and often with all board members are all strategies that help to strengthen ongoing and new relationships. Even with all good intentions and much work, retaining a superintendent position is never a guarantee. The superintendent who understands the dynamics of the school board–superintendent relationship can better read the signs of waning interest.

READ THE SIGNS

In rare but memorable instances, a superintendent may be caught totally off guard by school board action to terminate or nonrenew his/her contract. Fortunately, most superintendents have some sense that they should be looking for another position before school board action is taken. This "feeling" may come from the school board or from the superintendent himself or herself. The signs may or may not be justified, but, nonetheless, if the signs are there, many astute superintendents take proactive measures (like searching for another position) to protect themselves. Some signs of dissatisfaction with the relationship may include:

- Frequent rejection of the superintendent's recommendations
- Increasing dissatisfaction with information or recommendations
- Changes in the tone and operation of the school board created by board member turnover
- Reversal of school board decisions at subsequent meetings
- Poor or "picky" superintendent evaluations
- Constant disagreement between the superintendent and one or more board members
- Community or staff petitions protesting a decision by the school board or a decision by the superintendent
- Media attacks
- Resistance to needed change initiatives
- A noticeable change in the overall climate of the district
- A sense that no amount of relationship building with one or more board members can change the tension at the board table
- Public comment by a school board member about dissatisfaction with the superintendent's decision or recommendation
- Split votes on critical issues
- Block votes on nearly all issues (same board members for and same against)
- Increased media presence at school board meetings
- Staff vote of no confidence

Superintendent performance evaluation is not the only reason a superintendent feels the need to transition to another position. In fact, given the nature of school business today, special interest groups, union pressure, school board member turnover, and single-issue disagreements are also common reasons why a superintendent's contract is not renewed or the superintendent leaves a district. It is just as likely a superintendent chooses to transition as it is that the school board makes the choice for him/her.

ESSENCE OF SEEKING, RETAINING, AND TRANSITIONING POSITIONS

The shortage of superintendents is both a bane and a blessing for those seeking a position in public schools. More choices allow candidates to spend time assessing the best fit or match with a prospective district. On the other hand, more openings in the superintendency increase competition for candidates and encourage rigorous recruitment. This recruitment process leads to shorter position tenure and less stability/consistency for school districts.

When seeking a position, candidates should research the district and the school community. He/she must come to the interview prepared with information about the district. A candidate should prepare a list of questions about the district that he/she asks school board members or other committee members in order to learn more about the district and its culture, values, and priorities. Remember that relationships matter—especially the school board and superintendent relationship. Knowing when to move on is sometimes not easy or desired, but it can be the best outcome for both the superintendent and the school board.

TIPS AND ADVICE

Tip: Pay Attention to Gut Feelings

Once the decision is made to seek a superintendent position, realize that not every opening is a good match with the skills and abilities a candidate can bring to the district.

Example:

An assistant superintendent in a large metropolitan district was ready to begin the pursuit of a superintendent position. His last child had graduated from high school and he had been in the metro area for twelve years—eight as a principal and four as an assistant superintendent for Curriculum and Instruction K-12. A colleague who was a superintendent in a small rural district called him and said he was leaving that position to take a superintendency in the metro area and thought that the assistant superintendent should apply for the vacated opening. Flattered that his colleague would think he was a good candidate for the position, he completed the application materials and submitted them to the search-consulting firm.

He was soon contacted and asked to come to the district for an interview. At that point he was told he was one of six finalists. This was certainly a surprise since he really was an "unknown" in the pool of superintendent candidates but, again, he was flattered.

He and his spouse arrived a little early in the community to take a look around prior to the interview. Because neither had been in this particular region of the state before, both the applicant and his spouse were very disappointed with the location and the look of the community. It was very rural and isolated. Having always lived and worked in or near large cities, they felt this was a culture adjustment. As they drove around the "town," both were trying to find positives about the area, saying things like, "Maybe we could build a home in the woods or on a lake in the area," or, "It really isn't that far from the nearest large city" (one hundred miles).

The interview took place on a Thursday. Once they were home, the candidate was almost relieved to have not heard anything from the search consultant or the district over the weekend. He went to work on Monday morning as usual. About 8:30 in the morning the superintendent's secretary came to his office and said that two school board members from the district in which he had interviewed the week before were in the superintendent's office. When the assistant superintendent asked why they were there, the secretary said they were doing a site visit and wanted a list of people to talk to about him.

He was upset by this and immediately called the search consultant and said he withdrew his name as a candidate in that search. The search consultant became angry and said he shouldn't withdraw because he was the candidate of choice for the position.

The assistant superintendent still withdrew his name from consideration. He felt that at least the board members could have stopped by his office to say that they were there or that he could have had some contact about the visit prior to the board members' arrival. The process and the lack of personal contact from the board members caused the assistant superintendent to develop a "cold" feel for the board and the district. This was enough reason for him to withdraw.

Advice:

Do some research about the district, and, if possible, visit the community before applying. The search process should be respectful among all persons involved. Sometimes "gut level" feelings need to be listened to.

Tip: Know the Facts Before Speaking to the Press

Sometimes superintendents believe that their skills and abilities would be a good match for any district, large or small. They may forget that every district has unique features that may require skills or background experiences different from those needed in their current district. Success, however defined, in one district does not assure success in another district.

Example:

A superintendent candidate for a large, highly diverse district was confident in his ability to take on the job starting day one. Over the previous six years, he had served as superintendent of an 800-pupil rural district and a superintendent of a 3,000-pupil, fourth-ring suburban district. He applied for the superintendency of a large (12,000 students), highly diverse (38 percent minority with three major ethnic groups) district. He was selected for the position.

Within the first month of his tenure, a group of vocal parents came to the school board meeting to protest treatment of their minority children in one of the district's two high schools. The school board meetings were televised, so the parent protest attracted much attention and media coverage. The superintendent was interviewed at the school board meeting and also later in the week; the issue became more prominent in the newspapers. The new superintendent was not used to having his comments nor his decisions scrutinized so carefully. For example, at a school board meeting the superintendent commented that he was "certain that there had been a misunderstanding and that once the parents knew the facts, they would understand." The superintendent did not realize that the issue of how students were treated in the high school was ongoing. The school board and the administration had been working diligently to investigate and remediate the concerns, but another incident caused an eruption of emotions. The superintendent wanted to avoid further contact with the press because of the volatile nature of the situation. He told his administrative assistant to tell the reporter that he had no comment until further notice. This angered the education reporter, so she became rather ruthless in her pursuit of the superintendent both in person and in the paper. The superintendent grew more and more defensive, and on one occasion in his office, he swore at the reporter. Needless to say the media battle had begun. The local press embarked on a mission to rid the district of this superintendent.

Eventually, after three long and difficult years, they were successful.

Advice:

Do not comment on issues before the facts are known, do not patronize angry parents, and do not get into battles with people who buy ink by the barrel.

Tip: Chose Battles Carefully but Always Take the High Road

School board elections can have significant meaning for some superintendents. Depending on who is elected and why, the election may prompt the superintendent to leave the district and seek a superintendency elsewhere.

Example:

A long-term superintendent (eight years) had a relatively positive image within the school community. He had seen the district through growing pains and had been successful in asking the public for additional building space when needed. As in many districts, limited funds plagued the district. On two occasions, operating referendums were brought to the public for consideration. One was approved, and one failed. The growth in student population created some challenges in changing demographics but, for the most part, the parents, students, and staff were working together to meet student needs. The superintendent was respected by his administrative team with few, if any, disagreements.

During the course of day-to-day operations, the superintendent became involved with a personal issue that had escalated and ultimately arrived at the superintendent's desk for resolution. The employee was a coach and a substitute teacher in the district. The person was recommended for termination by the activities director due to a poor attitude and disrespectful behavior toward some of the athletes (calling names, swearing). The employee claimed that he was justified in his behavior because the students were so disruptive. The employee recruited some parents and former students to attend a school board meeting to protest his possible termination. The issue was brought to the school board for their action. The superintendent recommended the termination, and the school board approved the recommendation.

The termination action took place in August, just a few days before the deadline for filing for the school board elections. The employee, now angry and out for revenge, filed as a candidate for the upcoming school board elections. The employee publicly ran on the platform that he would force the superintendent out of the district. The former district employee won a seat on the school board.

Less than one month after the election, the superintendent announced his resignation effective at the end of the school year. The superintendent publicly stated that he was resigning because of derogatory comments made by this former employee toward him and his superintendency. The majority of the district residents and employees did not want the superintendent to leave. Even the newly elected board member said that he really didn't mean what he said in the campaign for the school board seat.

The superintendent did leave the district and was hired in another district in another state. He did not regret his decision.

Advice:

Sometimes there is an issue so important to the superintendent that it becomes nonnegotiable. It is a deal-breaker. There are many of these for most superintendents—chose carefully which is the "one."

Tip: Don't Overanalyze Rejection

The school board has the final say in who is hired for the superintendent position. One or more school board members may have a "favorite candidate" or be swayed by factors outside of the application, interview, and selection process. If not selected for the position, there may or may not be "politics" at work, so move on; don't try to second-guess all that happened. It is not a good use of time.

Example:

An assistant superintendent in a large suburban district was encouraged to apply for a superintendent position in the same state but in a smaller district one hundred miles south of where she currently worked. She researched the district and determined that it would be a place she could enjoy and that her strengths seemed to match well with those listed as desired in the posting. Of particular interest was the emphasis on curriculum and instructional leadership since that was her strength. She contacted the search consultant, submitted materials, and met with the search firm for an initial interview.

The search firm appeared to be quite excited about her application and told her that of all the applicants, they believed she would be in the top three. She interviewed with the school board, with a community group, and with a staff group. At the end of the interview process, the search consultant said that she did a "splendid job" and he was confident that she came out on top in each of the three groups' assessment. He was there with each interview and spoke to the groups after the interviews were completed, so she believed he relayed an accurate assessment of the reactions by each group.

The next day the search consultant notified her that she did not get the position. The search consultant seemed apologetic and really could not relate a reason why another candidate had been offered the position, and in fact, said it was somewhat of a mystery to him. A few months later, the candidate heard through the grapevine (there are many grapevines) that the assistant superintendent in the district where she had applied for the superintendent position told the school board that if his favorite candidate was not selected, he would leave the district. Apparently, the assistant superintendent had been in the district long enough to gain some clout. The board certainly did not want to lose both their superintendent and assistant superintendent in the same year. There was a "little" rumor that the assistant superintendent had also said that he would not work for a woman.

Whether any of the grapevine or rumor mill issues were accurate or not, the candidate would never know. Since this was her first experience at seriously looking for a superintendency, it was not necessarily a positive one. However, she learned that if the conditions for being hired in a district are not ideal, then perhaps there is another position "out there" that would be better in the long run. This proved to be true for her, and she was hired the next year in a district that was excited to have her. That relationship lasted over a decade and was a positive one for her, the district, and the school board.

Advice:

Most superintendents today have experienced disappointment in seeking a position. Why a candidate isn't offered a position may or may not have a reasonable explanation. There are always other opportunities, and fortunately, many that are better than the one that got away.

Tip: Know When to Hold 'Em and When to Fold 'Em

Superintendents often know when it is time to transition to another position. In fact, some are well prepared for their next move. It is the wise superintendent who can read the tea leaves to know if it is time to transition.

Example:

There are three major circumstances (among probably hundreds) that may lead to a superintendent feeling that he/she needs to transition to another position. These are:

- Irresolvable differences with a school board member
- Closing one or more schools in small towns that are part of the district
- Continued failure to pass needed referendum

The first issue can be the most challenging since a reputable superintendent truly does not want to take on a board member in public. As bad as the board member's behavior might be, the superintendent knows that diplomacy at and away from the board table is the only choice he/she has.

To illustrate the point, a superintendent began his tenure with unqualified support from each school board member. As the first two years evolved, one of the school board members seemed to need more "alone time" with the superintendent to discuss school issues. The superintendent became increasingly uncomfortable with the amount of time the board member needed. When she began to suggest that he meet her in her home for coffee to discuss issues, he began to make excuses to avoid such a meeting. He said that if a meeting was needed, his office would be the most convenient. If the board member did come to his office, he felt it was safest to leave the door open and have his administrative assistant still in the outer office.

As he distanced himself from her, the board member became increasingly agitated and angry with him. She began to attack him and his positions at the board table; she became argumentative on relatively simple issues. She questioned information he provided to the school board and attempted to portray the superintendent as withholding information from the board. In all of the interactions, the superintendent always took the "high road," never openly challenging the board member or publicly attacking her. Into his fourth year of tenure with the district, there was no question that the battle lines were drawn and would continue. The board member was obviously on a mission and only the superintendent, the board member, the superintendent's administrative assistant, and the superintendent's wife knew the whole situation. The superintendent submitted his resignation a year in advance.

The next school board election changed the board composition, but the superintendent had already moved on.

Advice:

One school board member can cause the stress level of a superintendent to rise beyond the point of being worth staying in the position. Taking the high road is always the best strategy for a superintendent, even when fighting back sounds like a better idea.

Quick Tips

An often-overlooked aspect of educational staff development is a program that enhances the skills of parents to assist and support their students. If parent involvement increases student success, then school leaders should spend more time and resources on developing this pivotal priority in every educational program.

Form a book club with the board members and/or the building- and district-level administrators. This keeps skills up-to-date and helps instruct their leadership group on their role.

Build anyway to improve.

Give your best always.

Succeed knowing that some don't want you to.

See the big picture.

Think systems.

Learn and understand the strengths of your staff; put them in the right positions, give them room to operate.

Spend time preparing for things that may never happen and obtain the answers to questions that may never be asked.

Pay attention to what is important: people, budget, teaching, and learning.

Communicate, communicate, communicate.

Take the job, but not yourself, very seriously.

We were selected/elected as superintendents, not supreme beings.

Humor, when well timed, often saves the day (or negotiations).

Be private in constructive criticism and public with liberal praise for good work done by others.

Write down, if you must, the anger you feel toward another, but file it away unsent. Rather, meet face-to-face to try to resolve differences.

Seek advice and counsel from a wide variety of sources before decisions are made; consider them all carefully, but in the end, trust your own judgment.

Leaders build relationships—and thrive because of them.

Never ask anyone in your district to do something you are not willing to do yourself.

Do a self-evaluation without board prompting.

Avoid socializing with school board members.

Have nonnegotiable core values that all should meet. These are:

Treat everyone the way you want to be treated.

Always do your best.

When in doubt, always do the right thing.

Never, never modify the truth or misrepresent matters. Few get into trouble by telling the truth, but many get fired for telling a little white lie for the greater good.

Keep balance between work and family. A person out of balance is not as effective as one who is in balance with life priorities.

If you make a mistake, address it immediately; there is a very good chance the sun will rise the next morning.

Seek knowledge from your predecessor regarding insights, information, traditions, and culture of the district.

The foundation of any good educational system is high-quality, caring teachers. High-quality, caring teachers want to, and usually do, work for high-quality, caring administrators. High-quality, caring administrators want to, and usually do, work for high-quality, caring superintendents.

Decisions should be made in consideration of:

Internal politics

External politics

Fiscal impact

Educational merit

Never underestimate the importance of, and the close connection between, community pride and extracurricular activities.

Remember, as a superintendent, everything you do is noticed by someone. All of your good deeds eventually come back to you in the form of positive community relationships. The superintendency is all about relationship building.

Listen to the whispers, and chances are you will not hear the shouts. It is critical to listen to the constituents on a regular basis, so awareness of little problems helps prevent them from becoming big problems. Meeting with the community members helps build trust; people appreciate the opportunity to be heard.

The expectations of the parents plus the expectations of the teacher equals the success of the student.

Take care of the "big issues," and often the "little issues" will take care of themselves.

Don't play favorites with your administrative team. Administrative team loyalty is affected when you do.

Develop and maintain positive professional relationships.

School system leadership is a challenging responsibility and a great opportunity. Beyond the preparation, expertise, and knowledge needed for the job, the greatest attribute a superintendent can have is courage.

Get involved with your community and schools. Be active and visible.

Take time to reflect on your performance and your leadership. Learn from this reflection.

Never underestimate the potential impact of unintended consequences.

The job is you, but it is not about you.

Be active in your professional association; get to know your colleagues.

Don't lose your temper; always take the high road.

Stand up for what you value.

Superintendents who regularly visit classrooms see firsthand what is taught, how it is taught, and how the students behave—all valuable pieces of information.

Pick your battles carefully. Be willing to go the distance on issues you value the most.

Lead transparently.

Always leave the office with a briefcase or notebook.

Don't ever say, "Don't repeat this." Whatever it is will somehow, someday be repeated.

Lead from the middle or behind, not in front.

Don't perseverate on battles not won. Move on.

Calm seas will not make an expert sailor.

Avoid writing letters to the editor to defend or respond to someone else's letter to the editor.

Speak using facts. Opinions carry little weight in a verbal battle.

Be decisive, not impulsive.

Never speak on a topic with a large group unless you know what you are talking about.

The person you treat poorly today may very well be your board member tomorrow.

School system leadership is a challenging responsibility and a great opportunity. Beyond the preparation, expertise, and knowledge needed for the job, the greatest attribute is courage. It is not a job of personal safety and security.

Avoid becoming a lightning-rod superintendent. Manage conflict well.

Superintendents put their jobs at risk because of communication (or lack thereof), not because they don't know the details of the curriculum.

Remember the kids.

References

Burke, W. W. (2008). *Organization change: Theory and practice.* Thousand Oaks, CA: Sage Publications, Inc.

Caruth, D. L., and Handlogten, G. D. (2000) Mistakes to avoid in decision making. *Innovative Leader*, 9(7): 86.

Collins, J. (2001). *Good to great: Why some companies make the leap . . . and others don't.* New York: HarperCollins.

Cottrell, D. (2005). *12 choices . . . that lead to your success.* Dallas: CornerStone Leadership Institute.

Cunningham, W., and Cordeiro, P. (2009). *Educational leadership: A bridge to improved practice.* Boston: Allyn and Bacon.

Danielson, C. (2002). *Enhancing student achievement: A framework for school improvement.* Alexandria, VA: Association for Supervision and Curriculum Development.

Drucker, P. (1999). *Management challenges for the 21st century.* New York: HarperBusiness.

Drucker, P. (2006). *The effective executive.* New York: HarperCollins.

Evans, R. (2007). The authentic leader. In *The Jossey-Bass reader on educational leadership*, ed. Michael Fullan. San Francisco: Jossey-Bass.

Fullan, M. (2001). *Leading in a culture of change.* San Francisco: Jossey-Bass.

Fullan, M. (2007). *The new meaning of educational change.* New York: Teachers College Press.

Gemberling, K., Smith, C., and Villani, J. (2009). *The key work of school boards guidebook.* Alexandria, VA: National School Board Association.

Glass, T. E., and Franceschini, L. A. (2007). *The state of the American school superintendency: A mid-decade study.* Lanham, MD: Rowman and Littlefield Education.

Glickman, C., Gordon, S., and Ross-Gordon, J. (2010). *SuperVision and instructional leadership: A developmental approach.* Boston: Allyn and Bacon.

Guthrie, J., and Schuermann, P. (2010). *Successful school leadership: Planning, politics, performance, and power.* Boston: Pearson Education, Inc.

Houston, P., and Eadie, D. (2002). *The board-savvy superintendent.* Lanham, MD: Scarecrow Press, Inc.

Hoy, A., and Hoy, W. (2009). *Instructional leadership: A research-based guide to learning in schools.* Boston: Pearson Education, Inc.

Hughes, L., and Hooper, D. (2000). *Public relations for school leaders.* Needham Heights, MA: Allyn and Bacon.

Jazzar, M., and Algozzine, B. (2006). *Critical issues in educational leadership.* Boston: Pearson Education, Inc.

Knoff, H. (2009). *Best practices in strategic planning, organizational development, and school effectiveness.* Project ACHIEVE. Little Rock, AR: Incorporate Press.

Kotter, J. P. (1996). *Leading change.* Boston: Harvard Business School Press.

Kouzes, J. M., and Posner, B. Z. (2002). *The leadership challenge.* San Francisco: Jossey-Bass.

Kowalski, T. (2006). *The school superintendent: Theory, practice, and cases.* Thousand Oaks, CA: Sage Publications, Inc.

Larson, C. E., and LaFasto, F. M. J. (1989). *Teamwork: What must go right/what can go wrong.* Newbury Park, CA: Sage Publications, Inc.

Marx, G. (2006). *Sixteen trends, their profound impact on our future: Implications for students, education, communities, countries, and the whole of society.* Alexandria, VA: Educational Research Service.

Maxwell, J. (2003). *Real leadership: The 101 collection.* Duluth, GA: Maxwell Motivation, Inc.

Mintzberg, H. (1994). The rise and fall of strategic planning. *Harvard Business Review* 72(1): 107–14.

MSBA. (2009). Toolkit for school board and superintendent. Minnesota School Board Association, St. Peter, MN.

Northouse, P. (2007). *Leadership: Theory and practice.* Thousand Oaks, CA: Sage Publications, Inc.

Razik, T., and Swanson, A. (2010). *Fundamental concepts of educational leadership and management.* Boston: Pearson Education, Inc.

Schwahn, C., and Spady, W. (2001). *Total leaders: Applying the best future-focused change strategies to education.* Arlington, VA: American Association of School Administrators.

Sergiovanni, T. (1999). *Rethinking leadership: A collection of articles.* Arlington Heights, IL: SkyLight Professional Development.

Smith, L. (2008). *Schools that change: Evidence-based improvement and effective change leadership.* Thousand Oaks, CA: Corwin Press.

Townsend, R., Johnston, G., Gross, G., Lynch, P., Garcy, L., Roberts, B., and Novotney, P. (2007). *Effective superintendent-school board practices.* Thousand Oaks, CA: Corwin Press.

Contributors

The following Superintendent of the Year Award recipients submitted Quick Tips, advice, and/or example scenarios for the book. Their expertise and wisdom helped to make the book a rich, practical read for new or aspiring superintendents. Many of the superintendent respondents provided multiple scenarios and tips. It is obvious that these experienced superintendents value mentorship and want to help others be as successful as possible. In conversation with some of the contributors, it was truly heartwarming to hear how much they truly care about education, their colleagues, and the important role educators have in assuring all students will learn. My thanks and admiration will always be extended to these award-winning superintendents.

Contributor	Award State	Award Year
Dr. Anthony Bent	Massachusetts	2009
Dr. Ted Blaesing	Minnesota	2001
Mr. Jim Cobble	Idaho	2009
Dr. Patrick Crawford	Pennsylvania	2007
Dr. Brenda Dietrich	Kansas	2009
Mr. Robert Dolezal	Nevada	2007
Dr. Donald Draayer	Minnesota, National	1990
Dr. Kenneth Dragseth	Minnesota, National	2003
Dr. Harry Eastridge	Ohio	2009
Dr. Richard Eisenhauer	Nebraska	2005
Dr. Dan Espeland	Wyoming	2007
Mr. Rick Fenton	Ohio	2006
Dr. Dale Gasser	Colorado	2001

Dr. Robert Gross	Minnesota	1991
Dr. James Halley	Rhode Island	2007
Dr. Don Helmstetter	Minnesota	2007
Dr. Gerry House	Tennessee, National	1998, 1999
Dr. Ben Kanninen	Minnesota	2005
Mr. Mike Lannon	Florida	2007
Mr. Harry Martin	Alaska	2006
Dr. Michael Martirano	Maryland	2009
Dr. John Morton	Kansas	2006
Dr. Larry Nyland	Washington	2007
Dr. Robert Olsen	Michigan	2007
Mr. Dwight Pierson	Iowa	2007
Dr. James Rickabaugh	Minnesota, Wisconsin	1996, 2008
Dr. Kevin Settle	Illinois	2007
Mr. Stu Silberman	Kentucky	2009
Dr. Frank Sippy	Connecticut	2009
Dr. Kim Stasny	Missouri	2007
Dr. Greg Vandal	Minnesota	1998
Dr. Eugene White	Indiana	2002, 2009
Dr. Jim Wilsford	South Carolina, National	1989

About the Author

Kay Worner was born in St. Charles, Illinois, and lived thirty-four years in Des Moines, Iowa, before moving to Minnesota. She lived in Germany for two years before coming back to the United States to attend Drake University and graduate in 1972 with a BSE in Education, Secondary Social Science. She received her MSE in Special Education from Drake University in 1975. She taught special education in junior high and high school for seven years in the Des Moines area. At Iowa State University, Kay earned her secondary and elementary school principal license and her Specialist Degree. She received her PhD in Educational Administration in 1986, also from Iowa State.

In additional to her teaching experiences in Iowa, Kay served as a special education coordinator and a director of Curriculum and Staff Development before moving to Minnesota in 1986. She was an elementary principal in the White Bear Lake School District for nearly eight years before becoming Assistant Superintendent for PreK–12 instruction in the White Bear Lake Schools. In 1997 she became the superintendent in a central Minnesota suburban school district, Sartell-St. Stephen District 748.

Dr. Worner received the Minnesota Association of School Administrators Kay E. Jacobs Outstanding Leadership Award in 1996 and the Minnesota Superintendent of the Year Award in 2004. During her principal and superintendent career, she was an adjunct faculty member in Teacher Education at the University of St. Thomas and an adjunct faculty member at St. Cloud State University in Educational Administration. Kay left the superintendency in 2005 to become assistant professor in Educational Administration and Leadership at St. Cloud State University, where she still works today.

Kay and her husband, Roger, have six children and sixteen grandchildren. They love the northern Minnesota lake country, fishing, reading, and time spent with their family.

Made in the USA
Middletown, DE
07 December 2020

26686437R00097